MW01062251

"Mr. Ramroth's experience an(covers everything from the hist(* complexities of the approach n* project objectives in today's design environment. Ramroth's bright mind and lucid writing style illuminate a clear path to success for the modern project manager."*

Adam O'Dea, P.E., FBA, Inc.

"Whether in a large multi-disciplinary A-E firm or a medium sized architectural firm like mine, the issues and lessons in Bill's book are right on target. This book should be required reading in schools of architecture so that the graduating students are better prepared for the realities of the architectural world."

Loy K. Rusch, Vice President MCM Architects PC

"In a clear, straightforward manner, Ramroth has authored a great resource for aspiring project managers. They will find the information well organized and extremely helpful."

Sarah Reeds, AIA, LEED® AP

"This book is an excellent reference for both new and experienced project managers. Bill Ramroth captures the essential ingredients of successful project management in a clear and easy to read format. This is a must-have book for anyone managing projects."

Kenneth K. Shuey, P.E.

"William Ramroth has taken the many facets of project management and created a very readable and worthwhile book. This is an essential addition to the reference shelf of any architectural firm."

John S. Reynolds, F.A.I.A. Professor Emeritus, University of Oregon

"Anyone who wants to understand the historic underpinnings of design management and its connection to contemporary techniques for controlling design should read this book."

Daniel J. Wright, Architect

PROJECT
MANAGEMENT
FOR DESIGN
PROFESSIONALS

WILLIAM G. RAMROTH, JR., AIA

This publication is designed to provide accurate and authoritative information in regard to the subject matter covered. It is sold with the understanding that the publisher is not engaged in rendering legal, accounting, or other professional service. If legal advice or other expert assistance is required, the services of a competent professional should be sought.

President, Kaplan Publishing: Roy Lipner
Vice President and Publisher: Maureen McMahon
Acquisitions Editor: Victoria Smith
Development Editor: Trey Thoelcke
Production Editor: Leah Strauss
Creative Director: Lucy Jenkins
Cover Designer: Sue Giroux
Typesetter: Caitlin Ostrow

Published by AEC Education
30 S. Wacker Drive, Suite 2500
Chicago, Illinois 60606-7481
(312) 836-4400
http://www.kaplanAECarchitecture.com

Printed in the United States of America

08   10 9 8 7 6 5 4 3 2

Library of Congress Cataloging-in-Publication Data

Ramroth, William G.
   Project management for design professionals / William G. Ramroth, Jr.
      p. cm.
   Includes bibliographical references and index.
   ISBN-13: 978-1-4195-2812-5
   ISBN-10: 1-4195-2812-2
   1. Architectural practice–United States–Management. 2. Project management–United States. I. Title.
   NA1996.R32 2006
   720.68′5–dc22
                                        2006015559

To Perky, Andy, Stephanie, Bunny, Ken, and Adam

Thank you for your help and support.

Contents

I never dreamed of being a project manager. I wanted to be an architect. Like so many teenagers with the same aspiration, I wanted to design great buildings. I never thought about project management. I had never even heard of it. If I had, I probably would have thought that it sounded boring. As a teenager, architecture was like art to me. I naively believed that every building was the result of the creative artistic genius of a single person. How wrong I was.

While many articles in architectural magazines still leave the layperson with this impression, few architects, engineers, or planners are fooled. They know that buildings, along with just about everything else in the built environment, are collaborative efforts. They are the result of the combined resourcefulness and creative energies of teams of design professionals. A design team may be initially inspired by the creativity of a single person, but the execution of the design involves the hard work, dedication, talent, and inventiveness of many design team members.

Design teams, like most teams, require a leader, someone to coordinate the team effort to work as a harmonious whole. An orchestra conductor is an apt analogy. An orchestra needs a leader, someone to determine and start the music, set the tempo, tell the various musicians when to start, stop, and play together in a pleasing way. While the orchestra leader is called the conductor, the design team leader is called the project manager.

About 30 years ago I began managing design projects. I learned quickly that the project manager actually controls many things simultaneously: the work process that brings about the design, the team of design professionals who do the design work, the cost and schedule for doing the design work, and even the project design itself. Project management is the pragmatic integration of these components. It requires timely decisions that are in the best interests of the client, the design process, the work process, the design team, and the project schedule and budget. Project management requires a balanced mix of art, science, finance, time-management, and people skills.

At first I had a tin ear for project management. I could not hear the subtle discordant notes that foretold potential conflicts or problems. As I practiced, however, I learned more about the practical aspects of the real world of design and the management of it. Soon I became sensitive to its many subtleties. I could hear discordant notes and spot the little problems before they became big ones. I could feel when things were going right or wrong. I learned to smell impending disaster and anticipate the taste of success—if the team could just do this or that.

A slang expression exists for the business development staff of design firms: *rock turners,* who, like crab hunters, comb tide pools turning over rocks in search of the next project. If business developers are rock turners, then project managers are *rock stackers,* carefully balancing the multifaceted components of a well-planned and executed design project.

This book will help project managers stack and balance the rocks. Or, using a different analogy, it will serve as a toolbox with instructions, explaining how to use the various management wrenches, pliers, hammers, and screwdrivers needed to properly construct and manage multidisciplinary design teams and projects. The book explains why and how the role of project manager varies among design firms. Because design firms are not all equal, the rules of project management vary among them. This book addresses the relationship between a design firm's management structure and project management.

This book also discusses the steps involved in planning the design work, the importance of establishing meaningful milestones, and the techniques for monitoring project performance.

It explains the importance of timely decision making and includes methods for establishing and managing the project team. It covers the different contract fee structures and how they affect the management of the design budget. This book also examines project scheduling, including milestone, bar-chart, and critical path schedules.

In addition, the importance of project quality control is covered and why quality-control procedures need to be a part of the project work plan and how to monitor quality throughout the project.

The book discusses client management. Yes, the successful project manager has to manage the client, too! It examines the characteristics of a good project manager and provides project management rules of thumb—general practical principles that apply to all projects. Finally, it summarizes the information presented in the form of checklists.

I wish to thank the many talented architects and engineers I have had the privilege to work with over the years. Particularly, I want to thank my first employer, Whitson Cox, FAIA, for giving me my first chance right out of school. "I need another Duck around here," he told me with a smile, shaking my hand, one University of Oregon graduate to another. I want to thank Frank B. Hunt, FAIA, and John G. Wells, AIA—Frank for keeping me on when business was tough and John for spending so much time with me, teaching me the practice of architecture and project management. I want to thank Richard Kennedy, PE (1909–1985). Through example, Richard Kennedy taught me the importance of professional honesty and integrity. I am convinced that ethical and professional behavior are paramount to long-term success as a project manager.

I want to thank my son, Andrew, who helped me with my research, and my wife, Persis, for her helpful suggestions and attentive editing, and the rest of our family for their support. Finally, I thank Pamela Brodowsky of International Literary Arts for her encouragement and advice.

T he construction of the Cathedral of Santa Maria del Fiore in Florence, Italy, began in 1296. Its first architect, the sculptor Arnolfo di Cambio (ca. 1245–1310), never had a plan for finishing it. He had no idea how to dome-over the enormously wide crossing (the area of the church where the nave and transepts intersect to form the Christian cross that is typical of all medieval churches). Nevertheless, he began building anyway. Maybe he planned on thinking of something as he went along. But he did not. None of his successors did either. For the next 125 years the problem remained unresolved. Nobody knew how to finish the project.

The administrative team overseeing the design and construction of the church, the Opera del Duomo, was stumped. So in 1418 the Opera del Duomo announced a competition with the hope of receiving creative ideas for solving the great puzzle—how to finish the dome of Santa Maria del Fiore. The prize was 200 gold florins. As it turned out, the winner also received the commission to complete the church.

The Renaissance genius Filippo Brunelleschi (1377–1446) won the competition. Under his leadership, the design and construction process for the magnificent octagon-shaped dome began. The dome was completed in 1436. All in all, it took a total of 140 years to complete the dome!

Today, no building project should start without a plan for completing it. And the project better not take 140 years to finish, either! The world has sped up. Today, performance expectations are very high. Clients and upper management of design firms expect every project to succeed. Few clients or design firm principals want projects to take a day longer than necessary. Literally, time is money. Today, most design firms assign a project manager (PM) to every project and so do many clients. The PM's job is easy to summarize: make sure the project succeeds. When it does, the client and design firm upper management are generally very pleased and eager to share in the backslapping and all the other accolades that come with a successful project. But, should the project fail and the finger is pointed, the project manager is likely to stand alone.

Managing design projects has never been more important or more complicated than it is today. The task of managing them falls squarely on the shoulders of the PM.

To consistently succeed, project managers need more than just competency in their particular areas of technical expertise, whether architecture, engineering, or planning. They need management and administrative skills, information, training, and guidance. Project management is a balancing act of the technical, financial, functional, environmental, and aesthetic parameters that affect the design of all modern building projects.

Not many students of architecture, engineering, design, or planning started out their schooling saying, "I want to be a project manager." Students interested in the design professions typically wanted to be architects, engineers, designers, or planners. Once graduated, they began working within their chosen profession. As they worked and gained experience and competency, they slowly moved up the professional ladder and were given more responsibility and eventually, their own project to run. Unfortunately, little, if any, of their education prepared them for managing projects.

This is how I learned about project management—by doing it. In a sense, I was thrown in the deep end and had to quickly swim or sink. Fortunately, I did not drown. Nevertheless, learning to swim while I flailed around trying to keep a design project afloat was not always a pleasant experience. It is much better, safer, and more rewarding for everyone involved—clients, firm managers, and PMs—for PMs to learn how to swim before they are left on their own in the deep end with a complicated project to manage. Project management needs to be learned, just like designing an auditorium or engineering a bridge.

It is easier to understand complicated subjects when they are put in perspective. Project management is complex and expansive, requiring an overall perspective to see it properly. It is an intellectual activity that melds theory and practice, built up over generations. Because the art and science of project management have grown over time, there may be no better way of putting project management in perspective than through a quick historical overview. So that is where the discussion will begin, with a short history of project management.

1

A SHORT HISTORY OF PROJECT MANAGEMENT

A good place to begin the history of project management is with its oldest documented failure. The Bible tells a story about a project management meltdown of historic proportion. Nimrod, the son of Cush, "was the first on earth to be a mighty man"; he founded a kingdom in the land of Shinar, where he built a city of brick, stone, mortar, and bitumen.

King Nimrod was an ambitious man with a very big idea. The crowning achievement of his city would be a great tower. Convinced that he was equal to God, he decided to build it tall enough to reach heaven so that he and God could meet face-to-face.

Nimrod summoned Shinar's best minds. A project team of design professionals was assembled. A gigantic tower was designed. Construction began and for a while, the design/build project went smoothly. Nimrod watched with pride and eagerness as his tower grew closer and closer to heaven.

As everyone knows, Nimrod never made it to heaven. The Tower of Babel (see Figure 1.1) was never completed. It ended

FIGURE 1.1   Tower of Babel

The "Little" Tower of Babel, painting by Pieter Bruegel, the Elder, c. 1563, Museum Boymans-van Beuningen, Rotterdam, The Netherlands. Photograph courtesy of Kavaler/Art Resource, NY.

in failure. However, it did not fail for the technical reason one might expect. Although the tower was built of bricks and stones, materials not particularly well suited for a skyscraper, the choice of building materials was not the cause of the failure. God, knowing a thing or two about project management, caused a communication breakdown among the team members. He confused their language, so that they could not understand one another's instructions and feedback. Clear communication is essential to holding design teams together, and without it the team fell apart. The project was abandoned and never finished. Communication breakdown is a major project management problem. Today, it still plagues many large and complicated projects.

Of course, the Bible does not use the term *project manage-ment,* nor does it dwell on the importance of effective commu-nications in managing large multidisciplinary projects. The Bible, after all, is more interested in building worthy souls than worthy buildings. Nevertheless, the Bible is clear: the inability of the design and construction teams to successfully communi-cate destroyed the Tower of Babel.

A breakdown in communication is not the only manage-ment failure associated with large and complex building projects. Building projects can go over budget or fall way be-hind schedule. They can fail for technical reasons. They can end in big lawsuits. Many other things can go wrong, too, in-cluding death by a thousand little problems or combinations of any or all of the previously mentioned reasons. All and all, risks are involved in the design of complicated building projects. Project management must reduce or manage these risks. Considerable management skill is necessary to success-fully maneuver through the maze of risks that can threaten large design and building projects.

PROJECT MANAGEMENT AND CLASSICAL TEXTS

Because people have been designing and building things for millennia, one would think that by now all the twists and turns would be ironed out—that centuries' worth of sagely writ-ten advice on the how-tos and how-not-tos of project manage-ment must exist. Surprisingly, however, this is not the case. In fact, no classical books about the art and science of design and building discuss or even use the term *project management.*

For example, the most ancient classical text on the subject is *The Ten Books on Architecture* written by the Roman architect Marcus Vitruvius Pollio, who practiced around 30 BC. Because his work is the only surviving treatise on design and building from antiquity, he must speak for all ancients. In his treatise, Vitruvius never used the term *project management*.

Nor is there any mention of project management by our second oldest source, the Renaissance architect Leon Battista Alberti (1404–1472), in his equally important treatise on the art of building, *De re aedificatoria*. In English, the work is commonly called *On the Art of Building in Ten Books* or simply Alberti's *Ten Books of Architecture*. Even the relatively recent 19th-century theorists of modern architecture Jean-Nicolas-Louis Durand (1760–1834), John Ruskin (1819–1900), and Eugène Emmanuel Viollet-le-Duc (1814–1879), never used the term *project management* in their writings. Durand and Viollet-le-Duc did, however, address some of the issues of project management in their writing, which will be discussed shortly.

PROJECT MANAGEMENT AND THE SPACE RACE

The reason the term *project management* is not found in classical texts is because the discipline of project management is not that old. Project management and its study as a science and profession is a phenomenon of the 20th century. As surprising as it may sound to architects, engineers, and planners, project management, as practiced today, did not originate with the design professions. Project management and many of its concepts are fundamentally Cold War phenomena. While some of its tenets were in use prior to the 1950s, project management traces its roots to the U.S. military and its reaction to the launch of the Soviet spacecraft *Sputnik* in October of 1957. The world changed considerably after *Sputnik*'s short trip into space and back down. The race to space was on. Modern project management is the brainchild of the Cold War and the space race.

In the late 1950s, the U.S. military and its various defense contractors began playing catch-up with the Soviet Union's missile and space program. The military, defense and missile contractors developed a series of management processes for improving the success rate of their large multifaceted defense and space programs. Many of the modern-day tools of project management are the product of the desire of the Department of Defense (DoD) and defense contractors to reduce the risk of project failures.

By the late 1950s, for example, the U.S. Navy's Special Projects Office had developed the project management tool called Program Evaluation and Review Technique or PERT. PERT was used to manage the immensely complex Polaris Missile Program. PERT is a process diagramming tool that uses rudimentary statistics or probabilities to calculate the durational ranges for various work activities, or tasks, based on best, worst, and most likely case scenarios. Today, PERT diagrams, or variations, are used for managing many large and complicated projects. However, the use of PERT in the design professions is limited. This is, no doubt, because of its dependency on statistics, typically not the favorite or strongest academic subject for most design professionals.

Soon after the Navy developed PERT, the military developed the work breakdown structure (WBS), a tree-like diagram or list of project tasks and subtasks with associated budgets and durations. Figure 1.2 illustrates a typical WBS tree diagram.

The design professions have embraced WBS wholeheartedly. Most design firms of any significant size require their staffs to use WBS codes when filling in their time cards and encourage or require their project managers to use the WBS method to plan, budget, and monitor their projects. Chapter 8 will look at WBS in more detail.

Shortly after the Navy developed PERT, the DuPont Corporation developed the critical path method (CPM). To perform maintenance on its many chemical plants, DuPont had to safely shut them down, perform the various maintenance activities, and then restart the plants. The process was complicated, involving many tasks that had to be completed in the correct order.

FIGURE 1.2   Work Breakdown Structure

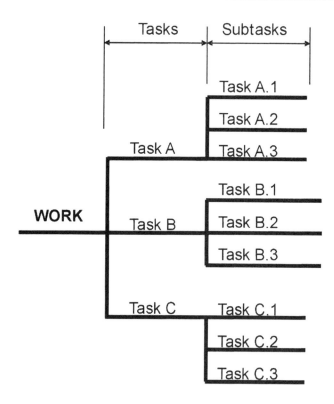

A work breakdown structure (WBS) is a tree-like diagram that breaks down work into its related tasks and subtasks.

DuPont developed CPM to manage the process. CPM is a network diagram that graphically shows a project, predicts the time needed to complete the project, and highlights those tasks that are critical to maintaining the project schedule.

The terms PERT, WBS, and CPM are just three of the many acronyms and abbreviations used in project management. For quick reference, a list of abbreviations and acronyms is provided near the end of this book, along with brief definitions for each.

Today there are a variety of computer software scheduling programs. These calculate and graphically display tasks, including the series of dependent tasks that have no extra or slack time slotted in their completion. In scheduling parlance, slack time is often called *float*. If any task along the critical path slips, the overall project schedule must, by definition, slip because there is no float in any of the tasks that occur along this path.

DURAND AND THE DESIGN PROCESS

Few project management techniques were in use prior to the 1950s. The process of planning existed, of course. Architects and engineers have been planning buildings, bridges, aqueducts, etc., for centuries. Vitruvius devoted many pages to planning temples, theaters, treasuries, country estates, town houses, harbors, and shipyards. Alberti devoted four of his ten chapters to the planning and associated ornamentation appropriate for various building types. But neither Vitruvius nor Alberti spent as much as a paragraph discussing how to manage the design process itself.

The first person to actually talk about the process of design was Jean-Nicolas-Louis Durand. Today, Durand is considered one of modern architecture's earliest theorists. Durand taught architecture at the Ecole Polytechnique in Paris from 1794 to 1833. Founded in 1794, the Ecole Polytechnique was not primarily an architectural school. It was a technical school, devoted to the education and practical training of two quickly rising groups of professionals, engineers and scientists. Between 1802 and 1805, Durand compiled his lectures into a textbook titled *Précis of the Lectures on Architecture*. The contemporary French architect and architectural critic Bernard Huet wrote that Durand's

. . . Précis is the first architectural treatise to take as its subject architecture itself, architecture without reference to building. For Durand, what counts in architecture is the inaugural act, that is, design.[1]

Unlike his predecessors, Durand talked about the process of design itself, not what buildings look like after they are designed. Prior to Durand, books about architecture were more like cookbooks with building recipes that were filled with descriptive texts and drawings illustrating the proper classical proportions and appropriate use of ornamentation for building facades. Vitruvius's and Alberti's books were two such popular source books. In addition, two other books by Italian architects were quite popular: *The Five Books of Architecture* by Sebastiano Serlio (Book Five appeared first in 1537; all books appeared in English in 1611) and Andrea Palladio's *The Four Books of Architecture* (1570; English 1715). All one needed to do was follow the recipes or copy the pictures and, presto, one created classical-looking architecture!

From Durand's point of view, the object of architecture was not to make classical-looking buildings. Durand thought that architecture had two much more important and practical objectives: composition and execution.

By composition, he did not limit the term to the proper relationship of ornamental elements needed to compose classical-looking facades. By composition, he meant the building in total, its functional composition, its interior spaces and their relationships to one another, as well. For Durand, buildings had a purpose beyond art. They must be practical and useful. He wrote:

> [F]itness and economy are the means that architecture must naturally employ . . . [T]o be fit for its purpose, it must be solid, salubrious, and commodious . . . [To be economical] the less costly it becomes. It is hardly necessary to add that, since economy demands the utmost simplicity in all necessary things, it absolutely forbids all that is unnecessary. Such are the general principles [of architecture] that must have guided reasonable men.[2]

Durand viewed design as a process directed toward a practical outcome, a building fit for its function, designed and constructed for a reasonable cost. Today, most building owners and clients would agree wholeheartedly with Durand: fitness and economy are important to a building's overall success.

VIOLLET-LE-DUC AND MANAGING THE MODERN BUILDING DESIGN

Durand did not lay out any specific procedures for achieving the fitness and economy he advocated. A generation or two later, however, another French architect did. The process he described included many of the basics of modern-day project management.

In 1873, Eugène Emmanuel Viollet-le-Duc published a book titled *Histoire d'une maison*. In English it is known by two names: *The Story of a House*, translated by George M. Towle (Boston), and Benjamin Bucknall's *How to Build a House, An Architectural Novelette* (London). Both translations appeared in 1874.

Viollet-le-Duc tells a fictional story about the design of a house by "Paul" for his sister "Marie" and her new husband. Paul is an amateur designer, but his cousin named "Eugène" (Viollet-le-Duc, of course) is a professional. Eugène agrees to give Paul advice.

Viollet-le-Duc's views on managing the design process are not presented concisely in any one place in *The Story of a House*. Instead they are woven into the novelette's thin plotline. While Viollet-le-Duc never called the procedures of planning and design he described "project management," he nevertheless explained the process of managing a modern design project quite well. Stripped of the plot and boiled right down, the house planning and design process that Viollet-le-Duc described is outlined as follows.

Identify the Need

What is the general purpose of the house? Viollet-le-Duc explained it this way:

> [Paul] must know what will be the proper thing for his sister. Shall it be a lordly mansion with towers and battlements, a cottage or an Italian villa?[3]

Viollet-le-Duc concluded that the purpose of the house in question was to provide a comfortable country home—not a city mansion—for a financially well-off but not ostentatious newlywed couple.

Develop a Space Program

Viollet-le-Duc had Paul's father say:

> You want to make the plan of a house for Marie; very well try it. But before all, it is well to know what your sister needs, how she desires that her house should be arranged.[4]

Viollet-le-Duc was the first architectural theorist to advocate the importance of developing a written space program, or "program statement," for a building project before beginning design. A program statement lists the required spaces (rooms) along with relevant design information regarding their size, function, special requirements, and relationships to one another. Viollet-le-Duc had Marie write to Paul:

> On ground-floor, vestibule, drawing-room, dining-room, office, kitchen not underground, billiard-room, study. First floor, [what Americans call the second floor] two large chambers, two toilet cabinets, baths; small chamber, toilet-closet; laundry, wardrobes, chambers plenty of cupboards [closets]; staircase safe from neck-breaking.[5]

Explore Alternative Plan-Schemes Based on the Space Program

Review alternative schemes and obtain client feedback/approval before proceeding with the detailed design. Viollet-le-Duc was a modern architect who believed in developing the floor plan first and then the exterior elevations. This was in direct contrast to the traditional (classical) architects of his time who concentrated on a building's classical appearance and symmetry more than the function of its floor plan. At one point Viollet-le-Duc resorted to clever sarcasm to drive home his point that a functional floor plan is more important than classical appearance:

> I know that a good many people are willing to suffer a daily inconvenience to have the vain pleasure of displaying, outside, regular and monumental fronts: but I don't believe your sister is one of them, and that is why I did not hesitate to follow what seems to me the law of common-sense, when we planned her house.[6]

The Final Design

The final design, including the exterior elevations, should be based on the functionally developed and approved floor plan.

Viollet-le-Duc does not begin addressing the exterior elevations or the details of construction until the floor plan is completed.

Learn from the Finished Project

Determine what worked well and what did not. In Viollet-le-Duc's final chapter, titled "The House-Warming," he had Eugène ask Paul for an appraisal of the house. The two proceeded to discuss the house and its rooms, features, and details as a critic today might analyze the features of a modern building.

The design process Viollet-le-Duc described in his story is relevant to more than just houses. It applies to all building projects. In general, Viollet-le-Duc's description of the design process coincides with the five basic steps in the process of designing any structure or building project. The steps are:

1. Identify the need.
2. Develop a detailed program statement for the project.
3. Explore alternatives that satisfy the program statement.
4. Execute the project based on the selected alternative that best satisfies the program statement.
5. Learn from the completed project: What went right and what went wrong?

Viollet-le-Duc addressed one other step often included in the design process. In his chapter titled "Criticism," he fictionally subjected the house design to what today might be called an independent design review. Viollet-le-Duc had the review undertaken by an elderly, opinionated man named M. Durosay, who had experience in house designs, was well traveled, belonged to several learned societies, and whose opinion was greatly respected by others. While Viollet-le-Duc made Durosay out as a bit pompous and no match for Viollet-le-Duc's own expertise, the idea of a timely review of a design solution by an independent reviewer is a good one. Today, it is common within design offices for projects in progress to be reviewed and constructively critiqued by others.

TAYLOR AND THE WORK TASK

Not until the beginning of the 20th century was one of the most important project planning tools, the work task, identified and studied. The American engineer Frederick Taylor

(1856–1915) was among the first to examine the productivity of labor in a scientific manner. In his 1911 book *The Principles of Scientific Management,* he analyzed laborers and separated their duties into elemental parts, or tasks. He looked at each task in detail for ways to improve efficiency. Taylor wrote:

> Perhaps the most prominent single element in modern scientific management is the task idea. The work of every workman is fully planned out by the management . . . and each man receives . . . complete written instructions, describing in detail the task which he is to accomplish. . . . [T]he work planned in advance in this way constitutes a task which is to be solved . . . not by the workman alone, but . . . by the joint effort of the workman and the management. This task specifies not only what is to be done but how it is to be done and the exact time allowed for doing it.[7]

Prior to Taylor, the only way to get more work done was to hire more workers and/or work the workers longer hours. Taylor figured out that productivity could be increased by planning the work on a task-by-task basis and by improving the efficiency of each task. By stringing the more efficient tasks together in a logical order, the overall efficiency of the work could be improved.

In addition, he advocated performing unrelated tasks concurrently to further reduce the time needed to perform the work overall. Taylor's assessment can be summarized into four basic principles:

1. Base work methods on the scientific study of tasks.
2. Train workers to perform the tasks rather than hope they will "catch on" by themselves.
3. Manage and monitor workers to make sure that the scientifically developed tasks are performed properly.
4. Spend as much time planning the work as performing the work.

Principle four was revolutionary. To many managers of the day it sounded counterintuitive: spend as much time planning the work as doing the work? How could that possibly get the work done faster and cheaper? Taylor, however, insisted that it could. He thought that management should work side by side with the workers, encourage them through what he called "harmonious cooperation," and smooth the way for them by establishing more efficient work methods through scientific analyses of the work process. Through the combination of scientific analyses, planning, and harmonious cooperation, work productivity could improve.

Henry Ford, a revolutionary himself, saw the potential of Taylor's ideas. Ford contacted Frederick Taylor and asked him to apply his scientific analysis to the Ford Motor Company's Model T production plant in Detroit, Michigan. Taylor watched the workers for countless hours and performed numerous time and motion studies. He determined the exact speed at which the work should proceed and the precise motions each worker should follow to do his particular task. Gradually, Ford made changes to the assembly line and by 1913 the Ford Motor Company had the first moving assembly line in the world.

GANTT AND THE BAR CHART

Shortly after Taylor developed and defined work tasks, the bar chart was invented. The bar chart was the 1917 brainchild of Henry Gantt (1861–1919), an American social scientist, engineer, and associate of Frederick Taylor. Consequently, bar charts are also called Gantt charts in his honor. A Gantt chart is a chart or graph with the horizontal axis representing a timescale. The vertical axis lists the work tasks. Bars are used to represent the durations of the tasks plotted on the timescale.

Bar charts are useful production control and scheduling tools. They allow managers to visually sequence and study the duration of work tasks in relationship to time and to each other. In addition, project milestones can be shown so that a project's progress can be monitored, measured, and graphically compared to key target dates and milestones.

FAYOL AND THE PRINCIPLES OF MANAGEMENT

In 1916, the French industrialist Henri Fayol (1841–1925) published a book called *General and Industrial Management*. The book earned him the title Father of Modern Management. In it he outlined 14 principles that he believed are essential to proper management. These are:

1. Division of work
2. Clear lines of authority
3. Discipline
4. Unity of command
5. Unity of direction
6. Subordination of individual interest
7. Remuneration (fair compensation for work performed)
8. Centralization
9. Scalar chain (hierarchical ladder)
10. Order
11. Equity
12. Stability of tenure
13. Initiative
14. Esprit de corps (sense of pride for the organization)

To adhere to the 14 principles claimed that the person responsible for management must perform five basic functions:

1. Planning
2. Organizing
3. Commanding
4. Coordinating
5. Controlling

The person responsible for project management is commonly called the project manager. Stanley E. Portny, PMP, defined "project manager" in his book *Project Management for Dummies* as:

> The person ultimately responsible for the successful completion of a project.[8]

Some design firms, however, split project management responsibilities between two or more people, either on purpose or as an unintended consequence of how the firm is organized. Nevertheless, this book will use the term *project manager* (or *PM*) as Portny defined it, to mean the single individual who is responsible for performing all functions of project management.

FOLLETT AND THE PRINCIPLE OF SYNERGY

Social scientist Mary Parker Follett (1868–1933) spent her life researching and writing about the management and organization of groups, industries, and public institutions. She published her insights in a number of books and articles. Among these is *The New State* (1918) in which she examined the group process and the development of creative ideas. Follett argued that the general goal of all organizations, whether private or public, should be to assemble individuals into coordinated groups that become better, more creative, and more productive than the sum of their parts. In *The New State* she used the example of a committee meeting to drive home the point that a well-organized group can provide better ideas than any of its individual members:

> Perhaps the most familiar example of the evolving of a group idea is a committee meeting. The object of a committee meeting is first of all to create a common idea. I do not go to a committee meeting merely to give my own

ideas. If that were all, I might write my fellow-members a letter. But neither do I go to learn other people's ideas. If that were all, I might ask each to write me a letter. I go to a committee meeting in order that all together we may create a group idea, an idea which will be better than any one of our ideas alone, moreover which will be better than all of our ideas added together. For this group idea will not be produced by any process of addition, but by the interpenetration of us all.[9]

Although she does not use the word, *synergy* is the process at work in the group meeting that Follett described. Synergy is the process phenomenon in which the cumulative effect of a group is more than the sum of its parts. Follett believed that complex problems were not solved by what she called the "mechanical aggregations" of adding more people to a group or team, but rather they were better solved by the subtle process of intermingling the different ideas of the team members.

For the project manager, creating and maintaining a work environment that fosters a synergic team effort is well worth the effort. It contributes enormously to a project's success. Chapter 10 will discuss synergy in more detail.

COMBINING THE TOOLS OF PROJECT MANAGEMENT

By the mid-20th century, these were pretty much the project management tools that were available. Collectively, they could be used to manage the design itself, manage the process of design, and manage the design team while monitoring project performance. The problem was, however, that they were scattered around like dust in the wind. The tools were not assembled or succinctly written down in any one place. Consequently, there was little consistency in the use of the tools.

Some organizations used some of them, others used different ones, and some used none at all. This was certainly true within the design professions.

In a nutshell, no universally used or recognized standards for good design management practices existed. Nothing explained how to employ the management tools in any harmonious, meaningful, or consistently useful way. Within the design professions, managers of design projects pretty much managed by the seats of their pants.

By the late 1950s, design projects were becoming more complicated. Most large design projects were multidisciplinary, involving the expertise of planners, designers, architects, and various engineers—civil, structural, mechanical, and electrical. In addition, design firms were becoming larger and multidisciplinary.

In the early 1960s, managers from various industries began experimenting with the management tools developed by and for the DoD and the space program. The design industry was among them. Project management was slowly becoming a profession.

In the early 1980s, an organization was formed called the Project Management Institute (PMI). The goal of the PMI was to research and collect the existent body of knowledge regarding project management and establish standardized procedures for managing projects across a broad spectrum of project types and industries. PMI published its first guidebook in 1983. Entitled *A Guide to the Project Management Body of Knowledge (PMBOK® Guide)*, it is currently in its third edition. *PMBOK* is a recognized standard for project management among many major industries throughout the world. Now a professional organization with members worldwide, PMI has established a project management credentialing program. Members who successfully pass the program are granted the title of Project Management Professional (PMP).

PMI defines project management as:

> ... the application of knowledge, skills, tools and techniques to project activities to meet project requirements. Project management is accomplished through the application and integration of the project management processes of initiating, planning, executing, monitoring and controlling and closing.[10]

The person responsible for the "application and integration" of the project management processes is the project manager (PM). Dr. Linn C. Stuckenbruck, a pioneer in project management theory and instruction and a past member of PMI, wrote that:

> The project management concept is based on vesting in a single individual [the PM] the sole authority for planning, resource allocation, direction and control of a single, time-and-budget-limited enterprise.[11]

PMI organizes its management process procedures into five "project management process groups." They are similar to the design process steps that Viollet-le-Duc described in *The Story of a House* more than a century earlier. PMI calls the project management process groups:

1. Initiating Processes
2. Planning Processes
3. Executing Processes
4. Monitoring and Controlling Processes
5. Closing Processes[12]

Today, project management is a recognized profession. Project managers run projects of various types within companies from many different industries. Sometimes projects involve creating new or unique products. They can be prototype or pilot operations designed to create better results or processes. They can be computer software programs. And they can be design projects: new buildings, bridges, power plants, dams, roads, city infrastructures, etc. It is this latter group that this book will focus on: how to effectively manage design projects.

THE NEXT CHAPTER

The next chapter discusses several project management basic concepts, including its pragmatic nature and its goals. In addition, it discusses the basic activities of project managers and the typical phases of a design project. As the next chapter shows, the goals of project management, the main activities of the project manager, and the phases of a project are constant and do not vary from project to project.

2

PROJECT MANAGEMENT GOALS AND ACTIVITIES

Project management is an outcome-oriented process. Whether the process was managed properly cannot be determined until afterward, by judging the results. Project management is, therefore, a pragmatic process.

The American philosopher Charles Sanders Peirce (1839–1914), considered the founder of pragmatism, gave a lecture at Harvard University in 1903. In it he defined the pragmatic method:

> In order to ascertain the meaning of an intellectual conception we should consider what practical consequences might conceivably result by necessity from the truth of that conception; and the sum of these consequences will constitute the entire meaning of the conception.[13]

Applying the pragmatic method to the concepts of project management yields the following: the meaning of project management's various concepts are determined by the outcomes they produce and these outcomes, in turn, determine the usefulness of the project management concepts.

Project management has a number of concepts or management tools. These include: project planning; breaking down the work into tasks; scheduling, budget, and quality-control strategies; project objectives; and project management goals. The last concept listed, "project management goals," is a good one to begin with because it is fundamental to successful project management.

Goals are the purposes of project management. They are universal and do not change from project to project. Goals are the general results that the management process should accomplish for every project. The project manager must chart the course, choose the project management tools that are most effective, and lead the project team toward achieving the goals. There are six project management goals:

1. To reach the end of the project
2. To reach the end on budget
3. To reach the end on time
4. To reach the end safely
5. To reach the end error-free
6. To reach the end meeting everyone's expectations

Just achieving the first goal, reaching the end, is not enough. All six goals must be met if a project is to be successful.

GOAL ONE: TO REACH THE END OF THE PROJECT

This goal may sound trivial or obvious. "The end," however, requires a little explanation. It does not simply mean that the project must "come to an end." After all, a dead end is an end, but this is not desired. No design firm, client, or project manager would choose a dead end as a goal. "The end" is not an impasse or an amorphous, arbitrary, abrupt, or ill-defined stopping point. "The end" has a very specific and well-defined meaning. "The end" means finishing the project while meeting its unique set of objectives.

The words *goals* and *objectives* sound like synonyms. However, in project management terminology, the words have different meanings. As already discussed, goals refer to the purposes of project management that are common to all projects. Objectives are the project outcomes or results that must be achieved for the project to fulfill its specific intended purpose. Unlike project management's six fixed goals, project objectives can vary considerably in number and kind from project to project.

Common sense suggests that the objectives of a college campus classroom building design project are quite different from the objectives of a college campus power plant project. The projects are designed and built for two entirely different functional purposes and must satisfy different objectives. While their objectives are different, their project management goals are the same.

Objectives produce outcomes that are measurable and quantifiable. For example, the campus classroom building mentioned previously has space program objectives that define the number and sizes of classrooms, faculty offices, lecture halls, student lounges, study areas, etc. It is rather easy to determine if the design satisfies these project objectives by simply counting the spaces and determining their sizes and functional relationships.

Other objectives, however, are a bit more illusive, subjective, and difficult to quantify and measure. For example, determining if a particular design fulfills the project's aesthetics objective is subjective. Nevertheless, it is important and meeting this objective is generally essential to a project's success.

Many clients have additional objectives as well. For instance, it is becoming more and more common for building design projects to include objectives regarding energy efficiency and sensitivity to the environment. Some objectives are process oriented, that is, some clients require design firms to make presentations to corporate and/or community user groups and review boards or prepare submittals for and participate in value engineering (VE) sessions, where the project criteria and project design are re-examined by a third party VE team that looks for ways to improve the project's overall efficiency and/or reduce its costs.

In the case of many building designs, local planning and community organizations often add requirements that must be satisfied if the project is to be built. These can include upgrades to local utilities, road improvements, off-street parking requirements, landscaping requirements, public transportation upgrades such as bus stops or bike lanes, art-enhancement goals, and storm-water detention requirements. There can be many other objectives in response to community social concerns. Objectives such as these contribute significantly to the meaning of "the end" and the effort required to reach "the end."

Although "the end" is the final destination, it must be defined at the beginning of the project—the project objectives must be identified and their implications understood at the outset. They define the road map that leads to "the end."

GOAL TWO: TO REACH THE END ON BUDGET

Every client and design firm manager expects their projects to conclude on budget. "To reach the end on budget" has two equally important but different meanings for most design projects have both design budgets and construction budgets. For example, the design of an electrical substation has two budgets—the budget for the design of the substation and the budget allocated for the construction of the substation. If the project is to succeed, the substation design and construction costs must stay within their respective budgets.

Getting to the end of the design on budget with a design that can be built within the construction budget does not happen by accident or magic. It has to be planned and controlled from the beginning of the design project. Without a plan to control design and construction costs, there is no practical way to know a design project's financial wherewithall or whether the design is progressing with respect to the construction cost budget. Only when the design project is complete will anyone know how much money was spent doing the design and only when the project is bid will anyone know its construction cost. By then, of course, it is too late to make adjustments and/or corrections to keep the project from going over either of these two budgets.

Chapters 7 and 8 will discuss project construction cost control and design cost control in more detail.

GOAL THREE: TO REACH THE END ON TIME

Time equates to money for most clients. Most clients want to know how long it will take before their project is complete and they can start using it for its intended purpose.

Time is money to design firms as well. The process of design is labor intensive. Most of a design firm's expenditures are in employee salaries. Consequently, most design project costs are labor costs. If a design firm has an average billing rate of $100 per hour and ten employees are working on a project, it does not take a rocket scientist to figure out that the project is spending its budget at the rate of $1,000 per hour, $8,000 per day, $40,000 per week! Obviously, completing the project as quickly as possible is important for the project's success as well as the design firm's success.

Consequently, a schedule is needed to properly execute all design projects. Project durations may vary dramatically from two weeks to two years and longer. While it might be possible to manage a simple one-person project with a duration of only two weeks without a schedule, it is not possible to properly manage a longer, multitasked project with many design professionals without one. Chapter 9 will examine project scheduling.

GOAL FOUR: TO REACH THE END SAFELY

This might sound like it should apply to construction projects not design projects. Nevertheless, safety does apply to design projects and it is not just construction sites that are dangerous. Many design projects require field investigations of one type or another. For example, in the early stages of many design projects, geotechnical investigations, surveys, hazardous-materials studies, field reconnaissance visits, and field measurements are required, and these involve performing work on project sites.

Many project sites are active workplaces and can be dangerous if people do not follow safety procedures. For instance, fieldwork in or around an abandoned building may expose design team members to potential hazards such as structural deficiencies and hazardous materials. It can expose personnel to airborne irritants, molds, fumes, and disgusting things such as rodent feces, bird droppings, and even the occasional decaying animal carcass. These can all be potential safety and health hazards if safety precautions are not taken.

Process plants, refineries, chemical plants, treatment plants, and rail yards can be extremely dangerous places if one is not trained in safety procedures specific to the particular industry. These industries tend to provide well-established safety procedures that must be followed by all the design consultants they hire. All railroads in the United States, for example, require contractors, including design professionals, to take a "contractor safety orientation test" before performing any work on-site. Railroads require everyone to understand their safety procedures, follow them, and wear specific personal safety equipment when working in and around rail facilities.

In addition, the proper design of facilities can significantly reduce the risk of working in the facility once completed. Design can have a great impact on making facilities safer places to work. Design professionals have a responsibility to design facilities that meet certain legally specified code and life-safety requirements. Many facilities require additional features to make them safe places to work, such as maintenance and process facilities. Safety and health concerns apply to the design of office buildings as well. In recent years, all design professionals have either heard or read about the phenomenon of sick buildings. Sick buildings are buildings where occupants are exposed to various forms of airborne contaminants as produced from the off-gassing of building materials that is often exacerbated by inadequate ventilation.

No one wants a design team member or an employee of a client to become injured or exposed to a health hazard. Consequently, all projects need to address safety, in terms of the design team performing the work and in the design of the project itself.

A plan is needed that establishes the safety procedures that are to be followed by team members during the design of the project. In addition, the safety features that are to be designed into the project must be identified so that the completed facility will meet the objective of being a safe place for its users.

GOAL FIVE: TO REACH THE END ERROR-FREE

This goal should really read "To reach the end as error-free as possible." No project is perfect. However, setting an error-free goal is more likely to result in fewer errors than setting an easier goal.

Quality is extremely important to design professionals. A project that is riddled with errors greatly increases the design firm's exposure to liability and, therefore, increases project risk. In addition, projects with too many errors lead many clients to look elsewhere the next time they need design services. Projects of high quality are great business development tools. Clients who are pleased with the quality of a project generally return to the design firm for additional work.

Chapter 12 will discuss quality control in more detail.

GOAL SIX: TO REACH THE END MEETING EVERYONE'S EXPECTATIONS

This is the most challenging of the six goals. It is also the most subjective, with the most diverse and illusive requirements. It is ironic, then, that it just might be the most important of the six.

British architect Kenneth Allinson discussed in his book *Getting There by Design* factors that affect the perceived success of a project. The discussion is based on research by B. Baker, D. Murphy, and D. Fisher, whose findings were published in 1974 under the title *Factors Affecting Project Success*. Allinson summarized the researchers' seven most important factors that affect the perceived success of a project. They are: (1) coordination and human relations; (2) budget, schedule, and technical performance; (3) project conceptual difficulties; (4) project organizational structure and management controls; (5) project budgetary constraints; (6) project importance and public exposure; and (7) team capabilities.[14]

Surprising as it may sound, Baker et al.'s findings showed that factor one, coordination and human relations, was significantly the most important of the seven.

> Co-ordination and relations: Team spirit, unity, human relations skills, enthusiasms, participation, etc. This factor is about four times as important as the seventh factor and about 50% more important than the second factor. [15]

Clearly then, project management's goal six, "reaching the end meeting everyone's expectations," is very important. Achieving this goal will have the biggest impact on the participants' perceived success of the project.

Clients, design firms, project managers, and design team members have differing expectations. A project that satisfies the client's expectations but results in serious friction between the project manager and various team members is not in the design team's or the design firm's best interests. Complex design projects require a coordinated team effort where everyone does what is expected of them and with respect for one another. Good design teams, like championship-level football teams, are better and stronger than their individual members. Poor design teams are only as strong as their weakest link. Design teams with members who have serious disagreements and fail to perform in a concerted effort toward accomplishing the project's objectives will not last long together as a team. If relationships among team members are strained or shattered, how well will they play together the next time?

Because the project manager is the team leader, it is the PM's responsibility to understand, respect, and respond to the various motivations of team members. The project manager does not have to fulfill the role of group psychologist, but the PM must know how to motivate various team members toward the common goal of meeting the project's objectives. This often means that the personal objectives of team members must be satisfied along the way.

For example, suppose a talented engineer-in-training (EIT) on the project team wants to become a licensed engineer (commonly called professional engineer or PE). Using the EIT to perform drafting duties or other tasks that do not fulfill his or her learning and training needs and expectations is likely to result in the EIT looking for another place to work. If the EIT is worth keeping, the EIT's professional needs must be met. Project managers must be aware of the team members' needs and try to satisfy them.

If the project is finished with the team in tact but the client is displeased with the experience, the project was not successful because it is unlikely that the client will consider the firm for another project. If the project is completed and the client and design team are happy but the design went considerably over budget, then the design firm is not likely to be pleased. If the project is completed and the client, design team, and design firm are happy but the project manager found the experience so painful and stressful that the PM starts looking for another job, that is not good, either.

Managing a project, as well as everyone's expectations, is a juggling act. It takes experience, education, and a lot of practice to properly balance all facets of a project for the benefit of both the project and everyone involved.

The balancing act is pragmatic, as the beginning of this chapter suggested. Project management employs a series of management and analytical techniques—project management tools—that are used to define, lead, and monitor the design process. If the application of these management tools leads to the success of the project, then the way the management tools were used was meaningful.

In the introduction to *Pragmatism and Modern Architecture*, which looked at how the pragmatic process works in the design of modern buildings, I wrote:

Architecture [design] is a juggling act of technical, financial, functional and aesthetic parameters. It is the pragmatic method that eventually brings these diverse design requirements into balance.[16]

If a project is successful, the project management activities that contributed to it were effective. If the project fails, the project management activities—or at least some of them—were not effective and, therefore, had no pragmatic meaning because they did not achieve the desired outcome.

THE FIVE PHASES AND SIX ACTIVITIES OF PROJECT MANAGEMENT

In project management, the term *effectiveness* means knowing what to do and in what order. It also requires knowing what not to do. Efficiency, which is often confused with effectiveness, is doing things quickly, without a lot of false steps and rework. It is possible to efficiently do the wrong things. It is better, of course, to efficiently do the right things in the right order, because that is most effective. To achieve this, it is important to know the different stages, or phases, of a design project and the project management activities that should take place during each phase.

Various general books about project management divide projects up differently. Some identify four distinct project phases: start, planning, execution, and end. Others identify five: conceive the project, define the project, start it, perform it, and close it. Because this book is about the management of design projects, it divides a typical project into the five basic phases that are common to design projects. The phases are:

1. *Start*—the project begins
2. *Planning*—figuring out how to perform the work
3. *Design*—the project's overall design is worked out
4. *Production*—preparation of construction documents and/ or other deliverables based on the overall design
5. *Closeout*—the project work is completed

Different fundamental project management activities should take place during the different phases if the work is to be accomplished in a logical order and the project is to be successful. The six fundamental project management activities are:

1. *Defining* the design project's scope of work, budget, and schedule—in effect, determining the project objectives
2. *Planning* the work effort so that the project scope of work, budget, and schedule will be met

3. *Directing* the design team as it does the work so the project objectives will be met while staying within budget and on schedule
4. *Coordinating* the efforts of the design team so that interdisciplinary information flows smoothly and at the right time
5. *Monitoring* the design team's work product and progress against the project objectives, budget, and schedule
6. *Learning* from the project—what went right, what went wrong, and how to improve performance on the next project

Note the similarity between the six activities of project management and Henri Fayol's five functions of management: planning, organizing, commanding, coordinating, and controlling, as discussed in Chapter 1. Fayol's terms *commanding* and *controlling* have been replaced with the less harsh and less authoritarian-sounding term *directing*. Project managers of design teams cannot afford to behave autocratically or dictatorially. This will be covered in more detail in Chapters 4 and 9. Fayol's *organizing* has been replaced with the more inclusive term *defining* because the project manager defines (organizes) both the project scope of work and the design team who will perform the work. One additional activity that has been added is *learning*. For project performance to improve from project to project, the PM must learn from each project and apply what he or she has learned to the next project to avoid repeating mistakes.

Note, too, the similarities of these six activities with the five process groups of the Project Management Institute (PMI): initiating process, planning process, executing process, monitoring and controlling process, and the closing process.

In effect, these six activities describe the primary job of the project manager. The first two, defining and planning, should be completed in just that order: define the project first, during the start phase, and then plan how to do the work during the planning phase. The third and fourth activities, directing and coordinating, are ongoing throughout the design and production phases. The fifth, monitoring, is a reoccurring activity. A project must be monitored periodically and its progress compared against the plan for executing it. The sixth activity, learning, is perhaps the most important. Every project teaches new lessons. Learning is a necessary survival skill for project managers for it is the only way to prevent past mistakes from reoccurring. The old adage "You cannot teach an old dog new tricks" does not apply to project managers. Project managers, regardless of how much experience they have, are always learning new things.

Figure 2.1 illustrates the relationship of the six activities of project management with the five phases of a design project.

FIGURE 2.1 The Six Activities of Project Management and Their Relationship to the Five Phases of a Project

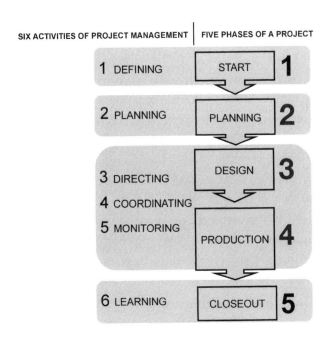

On a small project the six activities of project management are often obscured because the project manager wears other hats and may perform other activities—architect, engineer, planner, designer, drafter, writer, etc. These additional, yet very important, responsibilities take time and attention and frequently take precedence over other project management responsibilities. Frequently, the project suffers because of it. Even a small project requires proper attention to its management. There is a saying, "When you are up to your neck in alligators, it is hard to remember that the primary goal is to drain the swamp." The project manager must not lose sight of the primary goals of project management, regardless of everything else he or she is expected to do.

The typical education process of design professionals fails to prepare them for the challenges of managing projects. While similar in some respects, the project management process and the design process are not the same. University programs in architecture, engineering, planning, and design understandably focus on the vast technical body of knowledge regarding design and the technical information needed to practice a particular design profession. Few curricula address the art, science, and pragmatic aspects of project management. Consequently, most design professionals learn project management on the job. They learn it catch-as-catch-can by working with and watching other project managers, many of whom may possess limited project management and teaching skills.

Because teaching is not the prime focus of most design firms—design and production is—a common way most young project managers learn is by making their own mistakes, which are sometimes mistakes others in the design firm may have already made. In the previous chapter, for instance, one of Frederick Taylor's four principles of efficiency was to train workers rather than hope they "catch on" by themselves. Because the skills of project managers are crucial to the success and well-being of every design firm, it's a puzzle why the education and training of project managers is so often left to chance.

One of the reasons may have to do with the way some design firms are structured. Many design firms are set up in studio formats. Because of the organizational structure of the design studio, the responsibilities of project management are obscured, diluted, or shared between or among individuals. Remember the old adage, "When two people are in charge, no one is in charge."

The next chapter will explore the design studio and other common ways that design firms are organized. How design projects are managed depends on the setup of the design office. First, here is a brief checklist summary of this chapter.

CHAPTER 2 CHECKLIST

The six goals of project management, which are constant from design project to design project, are:

1. To reach the end of the project
2. To reach the end on budget
3. To reach the end on time
4. To reach the end safely
5. To reach the end as error-free as possible
6. To reach the end meeting everyone's expectations

All six goals must be satisfied for the project to be perceived as successful by all project stakeholders: the client, the design team, the design firm, and the project manager. The goals of project management should not be confused with project objectives that vary from project to project.

Project managers have six fundamental responsibilities. They are the six activities of project management:

1. Defining
2. Planning
3. Directing

4. Coordinating
5. Monitoring
6. Learning

Five basic phases are common to design projects. They are:

1. Start
2. Planning
3. Design
4. Production
5. Closeout

The project manager is responsible for planning the project work and running the project so that all six goals are achieved. To achieve the six goals, the project manager must perform the six activities of project management. Whether the project manager performed them well or not will be judged pragmatically at the end of the project by assessing their outcome. To this end, the project manager should ask:

❏ Am I planning, directing, and running the project so it can reach a successful conclusion?
❏ Am I coordinating the design team and monitoring its progress?
❏ Will the project reach the end on budget?
❏ Will it reach the end on time?
❏ Will it reach the end safely?
❏ Will it reach the end as error-free as possible?
❏ Will it reach the end with everyone satisfied and wanting to work together again because the experience was professionally rewarding and met everyone's expectations?
❏ What did I learn from the project and how can I apply what I learned so that the next project will run more smoothly?

3

THE DESIGN FIRM AND PROJECT MANAGEMENT

Managing a design project is not the same as managing a design office. As explained in the previous chapter, the primary goal of project management is to reach the end. A design firm's goal is to not end, but to keep going.

To keep a design office going, projects must end successfully. The greater the number of projects that end on a good note, the greater the likelihood the design firm will continue. If the opposite happens, chances are the design firm will not stay in business for long.

Historically, principals of design firms did not think of their practices as businesses per se, but as enterprises in support of their architectural, engineering, or planning interests, passions, and prowess. Design firms often focused on design to the detriment of good business practices.

Today, however, most principals of design firms realize that design is also a business and if they want their practices to flourish, or at least survive, then attention must be paid to the firm's finances. There is no better way for design firms to improve their financial performance and increase their longevity than by managing their design projects well.

The following illustrates why project management is so critical to a design firm's financial success. Suppose a design firm has five projects with fees of $100,000 each. Four of the five projects are managed successfully and yield profits of 8 percent. This equals an overall profit of $8,000 per project multiplied by four projects or a total of $32,000. However, suppose the fifth is poorly managed or not managed at all and goes 40 percent over budget. This equals a loss of $40,000. Overall, the firm has lost $8,000 on the five projects.

Ironically, the firm's project success rate was four projects out of five, or 80 percent. Imagine how successful a professional baseball team would be if it lost only 20 percent of its games. It does not matter whether a baseball team loses a ball game by 1 run or 20 runs. It is the same—one loss is just one loss. In the design game, however, losses are not equal. Depending on the size of the project, a 10 percent, 20 percent, or 40 percent loss on a project can be disastrous. One clinker can undo the success of many other projects.

It goes without saying, if the design firm folds, everybody who works for it is out of a job, principals and employees alike. Consequently, design firm principals (or partners, presidents, vice presidents, managers) and employees alike have a vested interest in how well design projects are managed.

Today, others are interested in design firm performance as well. Some design firms are subsidiaries of larger corporations that own multiple design firms, operating under various names with different design emphases. Some large design firms are publicly traded. For these firms, financial success often casts a large shadow over all other measurements of success. Publicly traded design firms tell Wall Street in advance how much money they plan to make. These predictions become stockholder expectations. If the predictions are not met, the stock price may suffer. Consequently, considerable pressure exists for the firm and its projects to succeed financially in the short run. Wall Street is much more interested in a project's monetary success than in any long-term artistic or technical accolades that the project or design firm may receive.

This does not mean that design professionals should concentrate solely on the bottom line. Design is important because the quality of the built environment matters to everyone. Architects and engineers are not licensed by states for their financial wizardry. They are licensed because they have demonstrated their competence and ability to perform professionally in a manner that protects and/or enhances the lives, safety, and well-being of the public.

For design firms to succeed on all fronts—financially, artistically, technically—effective project management is essential. Effective project management is the design firm's bread and butter.

DESIGN OFFICE MANAGEMENT STRUCTURES

How an office is structured greatly affects how projects are managed. This structure affects who is responsible for performing the six activities of project management and achieving the six goals of project management. An office's management structure establishes its culture. In *Getting There by Design*, Allinson wrote of office culture:

[Design] practices are action systems. What practices do and undertake, and the manner in which they do it is a rich matrix of many factors in relationship. This is "culture," which simply means "the way we do things around here," in that colloquial sense which embraces values as well as mundane activities and decisions.[17]

Office culture affects project decision making, timeliness of decisions, the quality of work, and how well the project budget and schedule are maintained and monitored. Therefore, it is worth taking a look at the various ways design offices are structured.

Design offices come in all shapes and sizes with different management styles. This affects the role and responsibilities of the project manager. In fact, it even affects whether there is a project manager or not! A small architectural firm with five employees manages projects very differently than does a much larger multidisciplinary design firm with hundreds of employees. Small design offices tend to have autocratic management styles, while large multidisciplinary design firms tend to be more democratic, more participative. Generally, there are four basic organizational structures for design firms. They are:

1. Sole proprietorships
2. Design studios
3. Multiple design studio organizations
4. Matrix organizations

SOLE PROPRIETORSHIPS

Sole proprietorships are design offices that are literally one-person ventures. Surprisingly, of the 25,000 architectural firms in the United States, approximately one half are sole proprietorships.[18] With some sole proprietorships, calling them design offices is almost a misnomer. Many work directly out of their homes.

Sole proprietorships offer many advantages. It takes little financial investment to begin most sole proprietorships. Day-to-day overhead is usually low. An obvious advantage is that the sole proprietor is his or her own boss. There is a wonderful freedom in setting one's own work schedule and pace and in determining what types of projects one wishes to pursue. Sole proprietors get to decide everything about both the design and business aspects of their practices. In a sole proprietorship, the design professional is the designer, drafter, technical writer, marketer, administrator, bookkeeper, and project manager, all rolled into one. He or she is personally responsible for a project's budget, schedule, design, production, quality, and success. Many design professionals like the freedom and control that sole proprietorships give.

Sole proprietorships, however, are generally weak project management organizations. The sole proprietor wears so many hats that projects often suffer from lack of project management. Projects are frequently managed without a written plan or strategy. Projects are executed by experience and instinct. Programs, schedules, and budgets are often kept in the head. Projects are flown by the seat of the pants.

There is a definite limit to the number, size, and complexity of projects that a sole proprietorship can successfully undertake. A sole proprietor's ability to meet client design expectations, liability, other insurance requirements, and financial stability requisites are limited. Should the sole proprietor have too many other projects, become sick, or decide to take a vacation, a client's project can suffer greatly from neglect. Sophisticated clients with complex building programs frequently steer clear of sole proprietorships for design services.

DESIGN STUDIOS

The design studio is the most common organizational structure for small to medium-size single-discipline design firms. Design studios vary in size from several employees to staffs of a few dozen or more. Although there is no set cutoff, once a design firm becomes large enough, for example, 40 to 50 people or so, it tends to transform into some other organizational structure, which will be discussed shortly.

In a design studio, the office and design projects are generally managed by the design studio's owner. For the purposes of this discussion, the studio owner will be called the "principal" and if there are multiple owners, "principals." The principal sets both the design and production methods either purposefully or by example. The principal's work habits, ideas, vision, creativity, likes, dislikes, and managerial strengths and weaknesses all interact to form the office's culture and design approach or philosophy. In addition, the principal establishes the office's approach to project management.

In her book *Architecture: The Story of Practice*, Dana Cuff, Associate Professor of Architecture and Planning at the University of Southern California, summarized an approach to project management common to principals of many design studios. The approach is autocratic:

> It's really a ritual of making buildings—that's what our process is . . . I can't spend the time to lead each person through the office philosophy. I have to take command. I'm not ashamed to say that's how the office runs now. We can have academic discussions and question the program, the design, and all that. But at some point, I'm going to say, "We'll do it this way." And then the argument should end and we should draw it up.[19]

I recall a similar incident working in a small design studio right after graduation. The principal had an idea to make one blank wall in a large conference room of an office building project a whimsical expression of his clever nature. He had made a sketch, which he shared with us in the drafting room. His idea was, using plaster, to make one upper corner of the conference room wall look like its wallpaper was curling off of the wall. Near the middle of the wall there would be a bulge, as if something were under the wallpaper. And at the other end of the wall, again with plaster, a roll of wallpaper would hang from the wall, as if the wallpaper hanger was not finished yet, and maybe was just on a lunch break.

Some designers in the office objected to the idea. A drafting room discussion ensued. Some expressed their opinion that it was kitsch or even a dishonest expression of materials.

Others thought it was corny, stupid, etc. One designer vehemently refused to draw the wall elevation and detail it. The principal listened for a while, but not for too long. Eventually, he firmly reminded us whose name was on the shingle. He "volunteered" a designer to draw up the elevation and to detail it. The designer did so, although not without a bit of grumbling.

Although the examples that Cuff and I gave are of small architectural firms, they apply equally well to small engineering, interior design, and planning firms as well. Small design offices tend to operate in the design studio format and they are generally autocracies, with power and authority vested in one individual. The autocrat can be charming, charismatic, egotistical, quirky, or an SOB. Regardless, one person is in charge of virtually everything—and everyone who works there knows it.

Figure 3.1 illustrates the organizational structure of a typical design studio.

FIGURE 3.1   Typical Design Studio Organization Chart

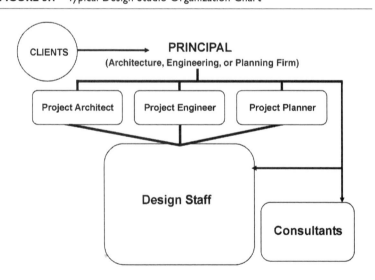

As Figure 3.1 shows, the principal is at the top of the organization and directs it. Working for the principal are project architects or project engineers or project planners, depending on the design studio. During this discussion, the initials PA will be used to refer to the project architect/engineer/planner.

In small studios there may be only one PA or none at all, with the principal filling the role of PA. In larger studios, there may be three, four, or more, but there can never be very many, as will be made clear shortly.

As Figure 3.1 shows, there are no project managers. In design studios, project management responsibilities are shared by the principal and the PA. How they are shared is often vague; who is responsible for what is frequently ill-defined.

Even when a PA knows what his or her project management expectations are, the PA often does not do what he or she thinks is best to fulfill them. Instead, the PA tries to guess what the principal would do and then does that.

Architect James R. Franklin in his book *Architect's Professional Practice Manual* commented:

> I found that once I got past the illusion I was a lone cowboy hero stomping out brushfires as soon as they happened and [past the other illusion] about being the quick-draw troubleshooter who had to make every decision [I realized that] too many times I was acting the autocrat . . . [and] actually providing the prime bottleneck, keeping good staff blocked from doing what the project needed and when.[20]

Autocratic organizations foster the attitude that it is better to trust the perceived gut feeling of the principal over one's own judgment. This serves to separate the PA's actions from his or her own judgment, an untenable situation that can lead to flawed decision making because it is often the PA who has the greater understanding of the project particulars that bear on a decision. When a PA tries to think like the principal but is unsure what the principal would do, decisions are postponed until the PA can clear them with the principal. If the decisions are time-sensitive, waiting too long can adversely affect the project.

Usually, few written rules and procedures are followed in design studio organizations. The PAs take their cues and direction from the principal verbally and/or by witnessing how the principal works.

This applies to the interaction of the principal with other members of the staff as well. I remember being an apprentice architect and watching in awe as the principal, on more than one occasion, sat down on my drafting stool. Using my clutch pencil and sketch paper, he deftly drew a three-dimensional sketch, showing me what he wanted me to draw in elevation.

In addition, the few rules or procedures that do exist are fluid. The principal tends to vary them depending on the skill levels of the PAs, the bond between principal and each PA, and the principal's idiosyncrasies and whims. In design studios, some PAs are more equal than others.

Below the PAs on the design studio organizational chart is the in-house staff who does the day-to-day design and production work. In small offices, staff members have varying and ever-changing assignments. Just about every employee is a sometime designer, sometime production worker, specification writer, cost estimator, illustrator, and model maker. Everyone pitches in and does what is necessary to complete the projects. With the right principal, the experience can be very rewarding for young and inexperienced design professionals, because there is little pigeonholing in design studios. Everybody gets a chance to do just about everything. Consequently, design studios can be wonderful learning experiences for apprentice design professionals.

However, long-term professional growth within a small office can be problematic. The autocratic structure of a design studio cannot support too many PAs because this spreads the principal too thin in the day-to-day operations. If the office gets too large, clients, projects, and PAs will not receive the adequate attention, direction, and decision making from the principal that is needed to keep the office functioning properly and the projects moving along smoothly. There is a limit to how many clients, projects, and project architects/engineers one principal can serve and manage without spreading the principal's attention too thin and thus become ineffective. Personal control is essential for an autocratic design studio to succeed. Once a design studio gets too large, its organizational structure must change or it may collapse because of its very nature.

For this reason, small offices frequently stay small. Project types and number of employees vary little. Employee turnover may or may not be high, depending on the principal. When times are busy, a few new staff members are added. When times are tight, staff is laid off. Over the long haul, the firm remains around the same size. Because of this, limited career advancement opportunities exist for employees within design studios. Many employees feel that if they want to get ahead, they must move on.

Principals of design studios often get personally involved in the design work, but this varies tremendously among principals. It even varies with the same principal, depending on the project. While many projects have personal meaning and interest to the principal, others do not. Also, the principal is often busy with other office management duties, which dilute his or her attention to the project. Consequently, the principal's input on projects is sporadic, poorly defined, and unreliable. The PA is expected to pick up whatever the principal does not want to do, does not have the time to do, or falls through the cracks. The PA cannot command the principal to make decisions; the PA can only advise. However, PAs can, and often do, manipulate information to drive the decision in a particular direction.

Some design studio principals bring their PAs along to client meetings. Others do not. Some bring the PA only some of the time. Consequently, a PA may not have the full picture of what the client expects and may not be privy to some of the nuanced requirements of the project program. Frequently, it is only the principal who knows all the pieces to the puzzle. In *Architecture: The Story of Practice,* Cuff told of a design studio principal's reluctance to bring young practitioners to client meetings:

> Henry [the principal] is not entirely unaware that he treats young practitioners the way he was treated when he was young. When he explains the delegation of design authority, he says he was not invited to client meetings for fifteen years, and does not intend to give rookies the advantage that took so long for him to earn.[21]

Like the sole proprietorship, design studios tend to have weak project management structures. The setup is much like the workshop/studio of a Renaissance master artist, where younger and less experienced apprentices worked on projects under the direction and tutelage of the master artist. In return, the apprentices learned the necessary artistic and technical skills and acquired the acumen needed to succeed in the craft themselves. The Renaissance master expected most of the apprentices to eventually leave and set up their own studios.

MULTIPLE DESIGN STUDIO ORGANIZATIONS

Larger design firms have found that the studio approach does not work well when numerous, larger, and more complex projects are all going at the same time and at different stages of development. In addition, larger firms must provide career path opportunities for their employees. Large organizations cannot afford to have the majority of their younger staff members continuously leaving. If these members did leave, the arduous process of training would constantly start over and never end. Training employees is expensive and requires patience and valuable time from more experienced staff. Also, team and organizational "memory" would be lost from project to project.

Keeping staff members who show promise is best for the organization. This requires offering interesting projects and career path opportunities.

Larger firms tend to have larger, more complicated, and more professionally challenging projects. These projects can suffer quickly from inattention. A principal spread too thin cannot effectively juggle the demands of numerous complicated projects.

The types of clients that larger firms seek out and attract are different as well. They tend to be larger private corporations, publicly traded corporations, or local, state, and federal agencies. These clients generally want to exercise tighter control over the function, design, cost, and schedule of their facility design projects. In addition, they expect design projects to follow certain standardized procedures to avoid unnecessary risk and uncertainties. Often these clients assign their own employees to be their project managers. Such design projects sometimes blossom into two projects running simultaneously—the project itself and the project paperwork that documents decisions and supports project progress.

Understandably then, larger firms are organized differently. One such organization structure is the multiple design studio office. This type of organization retains much of the historic allure of the design studio, but allows more projects to run simultaneously and offers more career opportunities to employees. As the name suggests, such organizations are structured as a series of design studios as illustrated in Figure 3.2.

Each studio is under the charge of a studio team leader. Depending on the firm, these leaders can be principals, partners, vice presidents, or employees with the leadership skills necessary to run the studio team. In this organization, each studio is more or less self-contained, operating in parallel with other studios, each with its own projects and staff. The firm can grow because more studios can be added, allowing the promotion of staff to fill higher-level roles in newly formed studios. Also, employees can move up within each particular studio.

FIGURE 3.2 Typical Multiple Design Studio Organization Chart

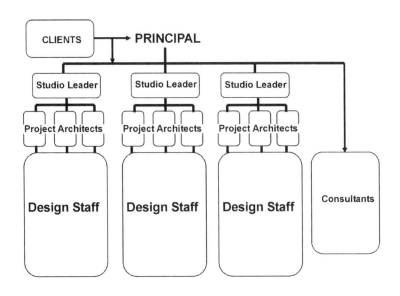

Like the single design studio model, this type of organization still has some of the same shortcomings. Project management responsibilities are shared among the group leader and the PAs and the responsibilities are often ambiguous.

MATRIX ORGANIZATIONS

Large design firms generally organize around some type of matrix structure. Large single-discipline firms employ a matrix similar to the one shown in Figure 3.3, while large multidisciplinary firms frequently use a matrix structure similar to the structure in Figure 3.4.

These organizations are called matrix structures because most staff members have different supervisors for different purposes. A member of a specific discipline has a discipline

FIGURE 3.3 Single-Discipline Design Firm Set Up as a Matrix Organization

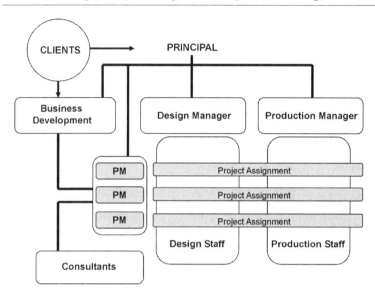

manager—sometimes called a department head—as a supervisor. This is the discipline staff member's functional supervisor. In addition, depending on the number of projects the staff member is working on, he or she may have one, two, or even more project managers as project supervisors. The intent of the matrix is to give total project management authority to project managers while maintaining high levels of technical competency and quality control over the work product. Also, the matrix offers numerous career path opportunities for employees, which contributes greatly to employee retention and project team cohesiveness. For these reasons, matrix organizations are sometimes referred to as "strong project management" or "full project management" organizations.

The matrix structure is by far the most prevalent of the four structure types among large multidisciplinary firms that employ scores, hundreds, and even thousands of employees and design numerous large projects simultaneously. Although the

FIGURE 3.4   Multidisciplinary Design Firm Set Up as a Matrix Organization

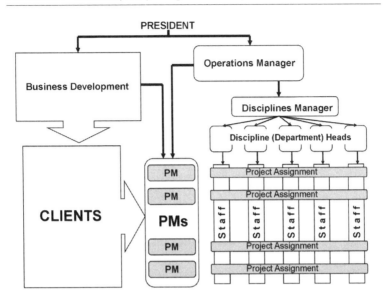

late University of Southern California Project Management Professor Linn C. Stuckenbruck was talking about projects, his words apply to large project office structures as well:

> The larger and more complex the project, the more likely that it will be multidisciplinary, that is, the project will involve many different areas of expertise. Complex multidisciplinary projects are likely to be organized in the matrix mode.[22]

The matrix structure is also the most complicated of the four, but as the British management consultant Peter W. G. Morris pointed out:

> Matrix structures provide for maximum information exchange, management coordination, and resource sharing. Matrixes achieve this by having staff account simultaneously

to both the integrating [project] managers and the functional [discipline] managers whose work is being integrated. Both project managers and . . . [discipline] managers have authority and responsibility over the work, albeit there is a division of responsibility . . . [23]

In matrix organizations, project managers are accountable for the performance of projects. In matrix organizations, there is no organizational-based confusion about who is responsible for project management. For this reason, many general books about project management and project managers begin with the assumption that the organization is set up in a matrix structure, whether it is a computer software or hardware company, an aerospace, oil, or chemical company, or a design firm.

While Figures 3.3 and 3.4 make it clear that all projects are run by project managers, the organizational structures give the PMs no clearly defined advocate within the organization. To survive, the PMs must form working bonds with upper management and multiple co-workers. PMs must attain and retain co-worker respect if they are to successfully lead design teams. In matrix organizations, PMs have full freedom to succeed and fail.

In Figure 3.4, note the vertical reporting and hierarchical relationship between the various department staff and their department heads. In matrix organizations, vertical reporting is functional while horizontal reporting is project-specific. Figures 3.3 and 3.4 illustrate this. However, vertical and horizontal reporting hierarchies within matrix organizations are not equal. Vertical functional reporting is almost always considered more important than horizontal project reporting. I have seen many multidisciplinary design firm organizational charts in my life. Virtually every one of them only illustrates the firm's vertical reporting structure, while completely disregarding the horizontal reporting structure that actually produces the firm's work product. One could stare at one of these typical firm organizational charts all day and never figure out from the chart how the firm actually does its project work.

It is not surprising then, that functional reporting within a matrix organization usually trumps project reporting. Generally, discipline members have more allegiance to their department heads than they do to PMs. In a matrix organization, discipline department heads hire and fire staff, not the PMs. Discipline members tend to relate more to their department heads because usually staff and department heads share similar professional interests. Also, the individuals filling the roles of department heads are constant, while there may be multiple project managers, with various skill levels. Projects and project managers change all the time. The department heads are more stable and this increases the bond between them and their staff. Generally, this allegiance is a good thing and causes no problem. However, smokestack or silo thinking can occur.

Silo thinking arises when a department head and his or her staff view their department as a little cottage industry, autonomous unto itself. This tends to hamper project team integration and can pit department head and/or department staff against the project manager. Usually, this is not in the best interest of the project. A matrix organization works best when all the members of the organization think first about what is best for the project, and not what is best for each individual silo.

Some multidisciplinary firms provide a supervisor for project managers. Figure 3.5 illustrates this, showing a management position called manager of PMs (other names are used, such as manager of projects). In organizations with managers of PMs, project managers have an advocate, someone on equal footing with department heads, who can speak for the collective needs and concerns of the project managers.

It should be clear by now that while the vertical reporting structure in a matrix organization is constant, the horizontal project structure is ad hoc. The truth about design projects is

FIGURE 3.5 Multidisciplinary Design Firm Set Up as a Matrix Organization with a "Manager of PMs"

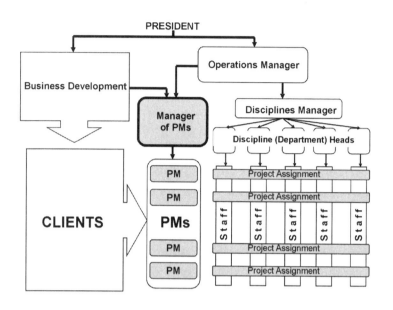

that they are organized into adhocracies. Kenneth Murrell and Mimi Meredith define adhocracies as organizations . . .

[e]stablished for a particular purpose . . . set up to deal with a specific situation and suggests that an action or group is temporary and flexible . . . used to refer to teams that form for a special purpose, across department or functional "lines."[24]

An ad hoc project team is assembled for a specific project around a single leader, the PM. When the project is over, the ad hoc team disbands. For the next project, the roles and responsibilities of various individuals may shuffle and coalesce again, forming a different team around a different PM.

This is the tremendous benefit of a large multidisciplinary design firm organized in a matrix structure. Its bench-strength of design professionals can be formidable, yet flexible. Individuals with diverse expertise can be organized and reorganized easily into different ad hoc project teams of various sizes focused around different PMs. Multiple projects can be run simultaneously with the same design professionals, their roles and responsibilities differing from project to project. While the project teams vary, the firm's organization is stable. This permits project performance to improve because the design team members' collective memories reside within the organization.

CHAPTER 3 CHECKLIST

This chapter looked at the various environments in which design projects are executed. Firm structure affects how projects are managed. Design firms are organized in four basic ways:

1. Sole proprietorships
2. Design studios
3. Multiple design studio organizations
4. Matrix organizations

Many detailed variations of these basic organizational structures exist. How the firm is managed affects how projects are managed. To successfully manage a project, the project manager must know how the design firm is organized and what is expected of the PM. The project manager should ask the following:

❒ Do I understand the design firm's organizational structure?
❒ Do I understand my position, responsibilities, and duties within it?
❒ Are certain project management responsibilities shared?
❒ If shared, who are they shared with?

❐ If shared, how are they shared? What are my responsibilities and what are the responsibilities of someone else?

❐ What decisions can I make? What decisions must be made by upper management? For example, can I, as PM, make commitments and/or decisions regarding design fees or contract modifications with the client?

THE NEXT CHAPTER

In addition to a firm's organizational structure, the way projects are managed is greatly affected by the abilities and character traits of the project manager. The following chapter looks at the characteristics of a good project manager.

4

CHARACTERISTICS OF A GOOD PROJECT MANAGER

Niccolò Machiavelli (1469–1527) would have made a terrible project manager. In his book *The Prince*, Machiavelli offered advice for a prince. He argued that because it is difficult to unite people into one like-minded person, ". . . it is much safer to be feared than loved." He explained why by saying:

> Because this is to be asserted in general of men, that they are ungrateful, fickle, false, cowardly, covetous, and as long as you [the prince] succeed they are yours entirely.[25]

He concluded that it is more practical to rule by fear than to spend time trying to win the love or respect of the subjects.

Whether this was sound advice for a prince of the early Renaissance is hard to say. But it certainly is lousy advice for today's project manager leading a multidisciplinary design team. The essential leadership characteristics for a PM are quite different than what Machiavelli had in mind.

To begin with, the project manager is not the project despot. If the PM behaves like one—ordering, threatening, and intimidating the design team—the project, the design team, and the PM, too, will suffer. Most design professionals are not ungrateful, fickle, false, cowardly, and best motivated out of fear as Machiavelli suggested. Multidisciplinary design teams are made up of well-fed, well-educated, and experienced design professionals who do not frighten easily and do not respond well to dictators. They perform better, indeed thrive, in democratic, participative environments where everyone respects one another and everyone is free to express their opinions, concerns, and creativity.

Although Frank Lloyd Wright (1867–1959) was talking about modern architecture's democratic style, his words, written in 1908, apply equally well to a team of design professionals responsible for the design of modern building projects:

> As Americans really demand of the architects a truly noble architecture, we shall never again have the uniformity of type which has characterized the so-called great "style." Conditions have changed! Our ideal is Democracy, the highest possible expression of the individual as a unit not inconsistent with an harmonious whole.[26]

PROJECT MANAGER SKILLS AND CHARACTERISTICS

Leading a democratic, participative, intelligent, well-educated, and creative group of design professionals requires a special array of capabilities. Not everyone has them, but a good project manager does.

A project manager must have a balanced composition of design, technical, organizational, financial, and leadership skills. A PM must know how to communicate orally, in writing, and graphically. A PM must know how to draw, at least well enough to convey ideas diagrammatically. Design professionals are visual people. They usually understand diagrams and pictures better and faster than they can absorb written words. For design professionals, a picture is worth far more than a thousand words.

Project managers must have the insight to know what kind of decisions they must make and when to make them. They must know what kind of decisions they can and should delegate to other members of the design team and when these decisions need to be made. They must strive for perfection, but be willing to make compromises because they understand that ultimately no project is perfect. They must be impatient but cautious in expressing impatience. They always want answers to questions sooner rather than later, but they must be patient when the answers do not come quickly. They must be tolerant and understanding of team members who make mistakes because they are still learning. PMs must be teachers, willing to take the time to instruct and nurture others on the design team who possess less experience and skills. PMs cannot allow themselves to be troubled by those little annoyances that always crop up in the course of working with others: somebody is late for work, late to a meeting, misses a submittal, makes a mistake, waits until the last minute, forgets to do something, or has commitments to other projects run by other PMs.

PMs must be courageous, willing to take on more and larger responsibilities. They must be willing to take calculated risks. Yet, they cannot be cavalier or careless with their decisions. Good project managers are plagued by thoughts about what they might have forgotten to do. They must always be on the lookout for the things that can go wrong. They must know how to avoid them when possible and provide a recovery plan should something go wrong. They must have a Plan B if it turns out that Plan A will not work (see Rule of Thumb 14 in Chapter 13).

A project manager must be able to look at the big picture—view the overall project from the perspective of 10,000 feet. Yet, when a team member seeks an answer to a small problem or needs a decision, the project manager must be able to zoom in, focus on the specific case, and give an answer, or know who can. A good PM must be the project's guiding sage and generalist.

Project managers must be able to think iteratively when planning projects and linearly while executing them. In general, an architect thinks iteratively, trying out design solutions over and over until the design is just the way the architect wants it. An engineer tends to think linearly. The engineer wants to do something once and then move on to the next task. Project managers need to think a bit like the architect and a bit like the engineer.

A good project manager must be able to manage more than one project at a time. Design firms often assign multiple projects to their PMs. A good PM can lead and direct multiple design teams working on multiple projects and switch his or her attention as needed from one project to another.

As an apprentice architect I learned to recognize and appreciate this skill. From my point of view at the time, one particular project manager seemed uncannily adept at thinking about multiple projects at one time. I recall one day he and the principal were about to leave for a job interview. The two of them had been in the conference room most of the morning preparing for the interview. A few minutes before it was time to leave, the PM came back into the drafting room. With one architect he discussed the such-and-such project, telling him that the mechanical, electrical, plumbing (MEP) consultant had called and needed updated floor plan backgrounds as soon as possible. He quickly checked the status of the floor plans and negotiated with the architect about when they would be finished. The two of them agreed that the architect would send the backgrounds by courier the next morning. The project manager then moved to another architect's desk to talk about a different project that was in the schematic design phase. He rolled out some tracing paper, placed it over the drawing on the architect's desk, sketched an idea, and asked the architect to explore it. He then came to my desk. I was drafting up redline comments from a senior architect. The PM reminded me that the project had to go to the printers that evening and asked that I phone the printers and tell them the size of the job, schedule it with them, and confirm that they could deliver it to the client before the end of the next day. By this time the principal was in the drafting room, chomping at the bit. He grabbed the PM and they were off to their interview.

The story may seem mundane but it illustrates an important point about managing multiple projects. Project managers must be able to redirect their attention quickly, from project to project and from a broad general view to a narrowly focused one. Not many people have the ability to switch gears so quickly, but good project managers do.

In addition to the general characteristics described previously, the following list summarizes the main must-haves of a good project manager:

- High motivation to manage
- Ethical and professional behavior
- Technical and legal competency
- Pragmatic decision-making skills
- Ability to make decisions with incomplete information
- A generalist's experience, education, and attitude
- Good communication skills
- Ability to empower a design team

The list is in no particular order. All these characteristics are important. The last one, however, has special significance because a project manager who empowers the design team truly unleashes a mighty force. What empowerment means and how it is achieved will be discussed in detail in Chapter 10, "Project Team Management." The others will be discussed here.

HIGH MOTIVATION TO MANAGE

Generally, people do best at what they like to do. Better project managers are the ones who like project management. In their essay "Leadership, Motivation, and the Project Manager," business school professors Dennis P. Slevin (University of Pittsburgh) and Jeffrey K. Pinto (University of Cincinnati) identified the basic characteristics of those individuals most prone to seek management positions. They called the characteristics "motivation to manage" (MTM) factors. According to Slevin and Pinto, highly motivated managers share the following MTM factors:

- Favorable attitude toward authority
- Desire to compete
- Desire to exercise power
- Desire for a distinctive position
- A sense of responsibility[27]

Slevin and Pinto suggest that would-be managers take a self-assessment test by rating themselves on a scale of 1 to 10 for each characteristic listed previously. The average is their MTM. According to Slevin and Pinto, those with MTMs of 8 or higher are likely to enjoy being managers. Consequently, they will do a better job of managing than those who score lower because the personal characteristics required to manage fit better with their personalities and aspirations.

ETHICAL AND PROFESSIONAL BEHAVIOR

"Do unto others as you would have them do unto you." This is the Golden Rule and the basis of morality for many religions. There is also a naturalistic, rational, and purely practical version of the Golden Rule called the categorical imperative. The categorical imperative was developed by the

German philosopher Immanuel Kant (1724–1804). It first appeared in his 1785 treatise *Groundwork of the Metaphysic of Morals*. It states: "Act only in such a way that you can will that the maxim of your action should become a universal law." Said another way, behave in such a way that it would not bother you to live in a world where the laws of physics made it necessary for everyone to behave the way you do. The categorical imperative is a very earthly way of thinking about the practical importance of moral behavior.

Moral behavior, or ethical behavior, is doing what is right all the time, even when it is easy not to. Also, it is doing what is right even when there is tremendous pressure to do otherwise.

Ethical behavior is one of the two essential characteristics required for a long career in project management. The other essential characteristic is always behaving professionally. Sooner or later, a project manager who behaves unethically and/or unprofessionally will find his or her world crashing down. Design teams respect and respond dramatically better to the lead of an honest, fair-minded, trustworthy project manager who behaves and treats them professionally. They respond poorly to PMs who act otherwise, like poker players who are always looking for ways to take advantage of the cards dealt and whose degree of honesty shifts with the circumstances. So long as this latter bunch of PMs maintain control through the power of their position and do not trip up, they can generally hold the design team, the client, and the firm's upper management at bay. But should they slip, their fall can be hard.

Ethical and professional behavior begins by understanding that project managers are first and foremost design professionals. They are not ruthless businesspeople who develop devious schemes or take corner-cutting measures to improve their own well-being or their project's bottom line. Project managers are not hustlers out to take advantage of unsuspecting persons or businesses who expect honest and professional behavior from their consultants.

The American Institute of Architects (AIA) and the National Society of Professional Engineers (NSPE) both stress the importance of ethical, professional behavior to their members. Both have codes of ethics and professional behavior and they expect their members to follow them.

In recent years, everyone has seen how dishonest, deceitfully clever, fraudulent, and nonprofessional behavior has adversely affected the honorable professions of accounting and the business of energy management. Understandably then, the AIA and NSPE have a strong interest in promoting and maintaining the ethical integrity of the design professions.

As the leaders of teams of design professionals, project managers should behave ethically and professionally and, thus, lead by example. Relationships with team members and clients are best built on sound ethical and professional principles. To behave otherwise shows a lack of respect for the design team, the client, and the profession. It also illustrates a lack of self-respect.

Following is a summary of basic ethical and professional principles, a code of ethics for project managers:

- The general public is the PM's ultimate client. At all times hold their safety, health, and welfare in the highest regard.
- PMs must know their personal strengths and areas of competency. They must also know their firms' areas of expertise and only provide services within their areas of expertise and competency.
- PMs should always behave in a way that honors the dignity of the design professions.
- PMs should never allow themselves or their design firms to become entangled with other persons or businesses that are engaged in deceitful or fraudulent practices.
- As licensed design professionals, PMs should only stamp and sign drawings, specifications, reports, or

other documents that were prepared under their direct supervision.

- PMs are the frontline representatives of their firms. As such, they must act as faithful, trustworthy, and honest agents of their firms.
- PMs should constantly strive to improve their professional skills and better their profession.
- PMs must not accept commissions, monies, perks, or favors from contractors or other parties that have dealings with mutual clients.

The last principle reminds me of something that happened many years ago. A contractor who was constructing a very large building that I was working on invited me on a golf outing. I was very happy to have been asked. I love to play golf and it was a great golf course, one that I normally would never have the opportunity to play. Even though the client, the contractor, and our firm had had a few spats and were involved in one at the time, I did not think about the impropriety of going on the golf trip. But my PM did. He tactfully explained to me the possible conflicts of interest, real or perceived, that could arise if I went on the golfing trip. I wound up not going. In hindsight, the PM was right, of course. From both a project and a professional point of view, it would not have been the ethical, professional, or smart thing for me to do.

TECHNICAL AND LEGAL COMPETENCY

Most clients seeking design services look for project managers who are educated and experienced in the lead design discipline that most affects the design of their project. If it is a planning project, they want a planner as the PM; an engineering project, an engineer; and for an architectural project, they want an architect.

For some multidisciplinary projects, it does not matter whether the project is managed by an architect or an engineer. For example, technical facilities that are designed around a complicated process system are very often managed by an engineer with expertise in the specific process. However, many other technical facilities with heavy engineering requirements are led by architects as PMs. Regardless, technical and legal competency always matter.

Architects and engineers involved in the design of buildings, facilities, and most structures are required by state law to hold specific licenses. All 50 states have licensing requirements for architects and engineers. States also license landscape architects and some license interior designers as well. Most states require that the execution of multidisciplinary design projects fall under the direct supervision of a licensed architect or engineer. The State of California's Professional Engineers Act includes a typical definition for direct supervision or what the act calls "responsible charge of work":

The phrase "responsible charge of work" means the independent control and direction, by the use of initiative, skill, and independent judgment, of the investigation or design of professional engineering work or the direct engineering control of such projects. The phrase does not refer to the concept of financial liability.[28]

Most clients of multidisciplinary design projects require PMs to hold licenses as either architects or engineers. The following is from a Federal Government National Park Service Task Order for a typical design project:

All site, architectural, and engineering work produced under this task order shall be performed under the direct supervision of a licensed architect/registered engineer . . . [29]

Generally, to clients, "licensed" means in the state where the project is built, not necessarily where it is designed, for many projects are not built in the state where they are designed. A famous example illustrating this point is the Seagram Building.

During the 1950s, the Seagram Company selected the world-renowned architect Ludwig Mies van der Rohe as the architect for its now famous Seagram Building located in New York City. Van der Rohe, who was living and practicing in Illinois at the time, was not a licensed architect in New York State. To resolve this problem, the Seagram Company brokered the collaboration of Van der Rohe and Philip Johnson, who was licensed in New York. While Van der Rohe designed the Seagram Building, many of its clean, crisp, and deceptively simple details that significantly contribute to the building's overall character—Van der Rohe commented that "God is in the details"—are the work of Johnson.

PRAGMATIC DECISION-MAKING SKILLS

As discussed in Chapter 2, project management is pragmatic. Pragmatic means that the effectiveness of any project management decision will be determined by its outcome, that is, by how well the decision worked. If the outcome turns out well, it was a useful or meaningful decision. If the outcome is bad, it was not a good or meaningful decision.

This does not mean that pragmatic decision making somehow gives the green light to unethical decision making. It does not. Decisions must be ethical and honest—always. In strictly pragmatic terms, the consequences of making decisions otherwise can bring about results that are devastating to both the project and the project manager. Ethical behavior is actually very pragmatic because it brings about results that are always defendable because they are principled, moral, and legally justifiable.

To ensure that decisions are meaningful, the PM must use the appropriate decision-making technique that is best suited to respond to the available information that bears on a decision.

Often this information is incomplete. Pragmatic decision making involves using all three inference tools of logic: deduction, induction, and abduction. Deduction is the inference that a conclusion necessarily follows from one or more general premises. Induction is the inference that a general conclusion can be drawn from one or more specific observations or facts.

While many people may be familiar with deduction and induction, few have heard of the inference tool of abduction. Ironically, everyone uses it. It is, by far, the most commonly used of the three. Whether they are aware of it or not, project managers resort to abductive decision making all the time. The reason is that most decisions must be made with incomplete information and abduction is the only inference tool that works when information is incomplete.

In *Pragmatism and Modern Architecture*, I defined abduction as the inference method:

> ... whereby a scientific hunch or educated guess, based on past experience, is used in problem solving. [Charles] Peirce argued that of the three [forms of inference], only abduction can be used to advance knowledge. Consequently abduction is often called "the logic of discovery."[30]

Abduction is creative educated guessing based on combining past experience with available information to form an inference that is likely, based on the available facts. It was the American pragmatist philosopher Peirce who first associated the word with the inference of logical guessing. Peirce explained that:

> A hypothesis ... has to be adopted, which is likely in itself, and renders the facts likely. This step of adopting a hypothesis as being suggested by the facts, is what I call abduction. I reckon it as a form of inference.[31]

If you carefully consider the question of pragmatism you will see that it is nothing else than the question of the logic of abduction.[32]

ABILITY TO MAKE DECISIONS WITH INCOMPLETE INFORMATION

Project managers rarely possess all the information required to make a decision based on deductive or inductive logic. Instead, they must be willing to make decisions with incomplete information. Decisions made this way are either outright guesses, which should be avoided, or thoughtful decisions arrived at through the logic of abduction. Consequently, most project management decisions are made abductively. Project management consultant Gary Heerkens in his book *Project Management* said that when asked to give tips to project managers he always says:

Learn how to make decisions with ambiguous, imperfect or incomplete information.[33]

To keep a project moving, decisions must be timely, that is, they must be made when they need to be made, not postponed until all the information is known. By then, it may well be too late to save the project budget and/or schedule.

In his book *Compendium Logicae,* the medieval scholastic scholar Jean Buridan (ca. 1297–1358) discussed the inadequacy of deductive and inductive reasoning to solve all problems. A clever story based on Buridan's work, believed to have been written by one of his contemporaries, has come down through history called "Buridan's Ass." It illustrates the absurdity of waiting until all available information is available before making a decision. In the story, a donkey is placed between two distant bales of hay. From the donkey's vantage point he cannot deductively or inductively determine which one is made of fresher and tastier hay and, therefore, constitutes the better choice to walk toward and eat. Rather than make a decision based on incomplete information, the donkey does not move and starves to death.

I remember a project where the mechanical engineer would not give the electrical engineer the electrical load information for a certain pump. It was a big pump and without the information, the electrical engineer could not finish determining the electrical load requirements for the project. The mechanical engineer's input was way past due, so I asked the mechanical engineer what the problem was. He said he was still deciding whether to select Pump X or Pump Y and he was waiting for more information from Manufacturers X and Y before he could make a final determination. Although the electrical loads for both pumps were large, the difference between the two was about 10 percent. Employing abduction—making a necessary and timely decision with reasonable-enough information—I said, "Tell the electrical engineer the load requirement for the larger one." His face lit up like a lightbulb turned on inside. "Oh yeah," he said.

Project managers must make timely decisions. Failure to do so can impede a project's progress. A project manager unwilling or unable to make up his or her mind when it is time for making a decision jeopardizes the project outcome.

A GENERALIST'S EXPERIENCE, EDUCATION, AND ATTITUDE

According to an old saying, "An expert is a person who knows more and more about less and less." If this is true, then a good project manager is the opposite of an expert. A good project manager must know a little bit about a lot of things. Because most large and/or complicated projects are multidisciplinary, the project manager must know enough about architecture, structural, civil, mechanical, electrical engineering, etc., to know how the different disciplines are interrelated and how each logically works playing off the work of the others. The PM must know enough to be able to hold meaningful conversations with design team members and understand their concerns, needs, and problems.

A good project manager is a generalist, which is the opposite of a narrowly focused expert. Generalists tend to be creative problem solvers because, to use an overworked phrase, they are more willing to "think outside the box" than a narrowly focused thinker and, to use another overworked phrase, less likely to "get wrapped around the axle" and absorbed in minutiae.

I started the Introduction of this book with a story about the construction of the dome of the Cathedral of Santa Maria del Fiore in Florence, Italy. Its architect, Filippo Brunelleschi, was a generalist, a true Renaissance man with the perfect credentials for managing design projects.

Brunelleschi knew something about very many things. He was a goldsmith, artist, sculptor, inventor, engineer, and architect. He was a self-taught practical man who learned and honed his skills through the process of hands-on tinkering, experimentation, careful observation, and abductive reasoning. This gave him the perfect qualifications for solving the variety of problems associated with the tasks of design and construction in the 15th century. For example, Brunelleschi developed linear perspective—horizon line, vanishing points, receding lines, etc.—to better study his architectural designs and anticipate the visual experiences of the people who would see and use his buildings. He vastly improved on the design of the hoist, designing and building a colossal rotating crane to lift and position the thousands of heavy stone blocks that formed the dome of Santa Maria del Fiore. He improved on the design of the scaffolding, including rest areas with kitchens up in the scaffolding so workers could take their breaks without having to descend and then climb back up to continue work. He designed and constructed an oar-powered barge to bring marble from a distant quarry to the dome's construction site. Unfortunately, it sank on its maiden voyage. Cargo and all were lost. Undaunted, he continued working in the same vein, confidently tackling and solving problems as they cropped up. Brunelleschi learned from both his successes and failures.

Because of Brunelleschi's approach to design, construction, and problem solving, the Cathedral of Santa Maria del Fiore stands as a bridge between two worlds. In 1296, it began as a typical late-medieval Tuscan-styled church. Brunelleschi finished it in a new style, as a fledgling example of Renaissance architecture.

Today, the management of multidisciplinary design projects requires a general grasp of the design process, the design business, and enough of an understanding about the construction industry to communicate effectively with members of both the design and construction professions. It requires a basic understanding of the disciplines of planning, design, architecture, engineering, and construction to speak intelligently, at least in general terms, about any design or construction-related subject with clients, design team members, and builders. It requires enough knowledge to correctly make the necessary decisions that transcend the often narrow focus of the individual disciplines.

Last, but equally important, project management requires enough understanding of the disciplines to know what one does not know. The truly wise project manager knows what he or she knows and what he or she does not know. The wise PM knows who to speak with to get the right answers and has the good judgment to make adjustments in the work, based on the greater expertise of others.

No one ever accused Frank Lloyd Wright of lacking confidence. "Early in life I had to choose between honest arrogance and hypocritical humility," he said. "I chose the former and have seen no reason to change."[34] In 1946, Frank Lloyd Wright's son, John Lloyd Wright, published a book about his father. The very title put JLW's relationship with his egotistical father in perspective: *My Father Who Is on Earth*. In 1949, at the age of 82, Frank Lloyd Wright received the AIA's Gold Medal Award, its highest honor. In his acceptance speech, Wright began by saying, "Well, it's about time!"[35]

Nevertheless, Wright had the wisdom to listen to and take the advice of those with more experience than he, if it would benefit his projects. For example, Wright wanted his famous spiral-shaped Guggenheim Museum to have both spatial continuity and structural continuity. He envisioned the museum patrons flowing down the ramp, uninterrupted by intervening floors, as they admired the modern art paintings hanging on the museum's spiraling wall. In turn, the ramp they walked on would flow, too, monolithically spiraling down, uninterrupted by any construction joints whatsoever.

In 1949, the museum project went out to bid. The low bidder was Euclid Contracting Corporation. Euclid's bid, however, was about 50 percent over budget. If the Guggenheim was to be built, its cost would have to be cut. Wright did not tackle the cost cuts alone. He wisely chose to work with the contractor to make the necessary cuts. Because Euclid was a highway and bridge contractor, use to building freeway on-ramps and off-ramps, it knew a thing or two about building concrete ramps. Wright realized this and listened. The contractor convinced Wright that it would be considerably less expensive to build the spiraling ramp in segments. This would make the concrete formwork simpler and less costly to support during construction. Also, formwork could be reused, again lowering costs. The contractor also convinced Wright to eliminate compound curves in the ramp design, making the task of forming the ramp easier. Wright listened, made changes, and modified the details. Wright's willingness to do so allowed his project to go forward and become one of the most recognized buildings in the world.

GOOD COMMUNICATION SKILLS

As the Tower of Babel story in Chapter 1 illustrated, clear communication is essential for the success of design and construction projects. Because most of a project manager's time is spent communicating, the ability to communicate effectively is very important. Ironically, being a good communicator starts with being a good listener. Remember Wright's willingness to listen to the contractor's suggestions in the Guggenheim story.

Many people do not really listen, including a lot of PMs. To them, listening is just staying quiet, waiting for the other person to finish speaking so they can talk again. They believe a conversation is a contest, a test of wits, and that the better communicator is the one who dominates the conversation. While the other is speaking, they are not really listening. Rather, they are planning what to say next.

But a good conversation is not a debate. It has no winner or loser. It is a mutually rewarding, constructive experience that leads to better project decision making.

Good communication requires active listening. Active listening requires focusing on what a person is saying and how he or she is saying it. An active listener does not interrupt, listens with an open mind, does not make assumptions, and tries to see things from the speaker's point of view. An active listener looks at the person who is talking and nods or gestures appropriately. Nods and gestures are visual cues to the speaker that the listener is actually paying attention. An active listener tries to understand and ask follow-up questions—without interrupting—to clarify.

Active listening improves a PM's ability to effectively lead the team because it increases rapport and trust with team members. It promotes decision making made with better and more complete information. This leads to fewer mistakes, because decisions based on better information are more likely to be the right decisions. Correct decisions lead to less rework, more confidence from team members, and a better project overall.

An active listening technique I have found very useful involves a pencil and paper. Most design professionals carry a pencil around with them as a matter of habit. I am one of them. Often when another design professional speaks, he or she is trying to explain something visual to me by using words. I listen carefully to what he or she is saying and try to develop a mental picture of what the person is explaining. When the person is finished, I may ask a few questions and then, to make sure I have understood what was said, I try to draw it and ask something like, "Is this what you are getting at?" Often the person will turn the paper around and, using his or her own pencil, finish, add to, or change the sketch. For design professionals, sketches are a wonderful communication and feedback tool. Pictures are worth ten thousand words to design professionals.

Of course, words are important, too. PMs must be able to communicate their ideas to clients and team members in words. Their instructions must be clear, so everyone knows exactly what is intended.

Oral communication is improved when the speaker looks at the listener, attaining eye contact. If there is more than one listener, the speaker should move his or her attention from one listener to another. Speaking benefits greatly from hand gestures. If standing when speaking, do not slouch. If sitting, lean slightly forward. Look attentive, sound enthusiastic, and appear confident.

At a company-conducted management training seminar I attended, one portion of the training session included a discussion of the proper and improper use of body language. The company was multinational with offices worldwide, and because the meaning of body language can vary among cultures, the company thought it was a good idea for its managers to understand the subtle meanings of body language. For example, arms and/or legs crossed or hands in pockets could be interpreted to mean the person is reserved and/or suspicious. If the eyes are downcast, then the person may not be interested in what you are saying. In some cases, rubbing or touching one's nose while answering a question means the person may not be telling the truth. (I have hay fever, so I've got to watch out for this one.) Good eye contact and a relaxed pleasant smile usually mean the person is receptive, open.

The seminar trainer told us that if someone is leaning back in his chair, with both hands clasped behind his head, it is interpreted as a gesture of superiority. She suggested we avoid ever doing this, likening it to the behavior of the dominant male ape in a group, saying it meant something like, "Here I am, see me, smell me."

Later in the seminar, the president of the company dropped in to talk to us and answer questions. He sat down, leaned back in his chair, and clasped his hands behind his head. It was all we could do to keep from laughing.

Meetings are an effective form of communication, assuming they are properly run. Meetings are the most direct way for the PM to communicate and interact with the design team as a whole. During the course of a day, the PM can walk around the office, talk with various team members one-on-one, phone others, share information, give direction, and make decisions that affect just the work of that particular team member. But if decisions require discussion, input, and buy-in from many team members, then a meeting is the appropriate venue. Also, it is the best way for the PM to share information that needs to be heard by the entire team.

Many people do not like meetings. This is probably because they have had bad experiences with meetings that had no purpose, took too long, accomplished nothing, and basically wasted everyone's time. A good project manager holds team meetings only when they have a purpose. He or she prepares for them in advance, decides what needs to be accomplished, what decisions need to be made. A good PM prepares an agenda for the meeting, distributes it prior to the meeting, and follows it during the meeting. A good PM starts meetings on time and ends them on time. One hour is a good length for a meeting. If a meeting drags on much longer than an hour, team members tend to get restless, drift off, and lose attention.

If some team members are late for a meeting, the PM should start the meeting anyway. Tardy team members will quickly learn that this PM starts meetings on time and they will be more punctual next time. If a meeting requires decisions, a good PM makes sure that those in authority to make or share in the decision are present.

Before the meeting ends, a good project manager summarizes what has been decided, what action items are to be taken, and who is responsible for them. A good project manager documents the meeting and distributes meeting minutes shortly afterward to all attendees and others who may have an interest.

A good PM is a good historian. It is essential to document project meetings and phone conversations. People's memories are short. A few months after a meeting or phone conversation, many people will not be able to remember what was said or agreed to. Decisions that were made may be forgotten because nobody wrote them down. Forgotten decisions are frequently revisited at some inopportune time, often causing rework. To avoid this, the PM needs to keep good records, which become a history of the decisions.

For example, I recall a building addition project where, early in the schematic design phase, a decision was made to not remove and update various existing pieces of building mechanical equipment. It was agreed that only the mechanical equipment affected by the addition would be upgraded. Many months later, during construction, the client wondered why a particular existing water heater was not replaced for it was ten years old. Although it had been discussed during design, nobody could find where the decision was documented. Nobody could find it, because the documentation did not exist.

In recent years, e-mail has become a very popular form of communication. It has its advantages, but it has disadvantages, too. Its main advantages are that the sender and receiver(s) do not have to be at their computers (or personal digital assistants (PDAs)) at the same time and the e-mail itself provides instant written documentation, which can easily be stored electronically.

Its main disadvantage is that there is no real-time communication between the sender and receiver(s). Consequently, the receiver can misinterpret the sender's message and answer incorrectly without ever knowing it. Some might argue that this is no different than writing a letter because letters, too, can be misunderstood and the turnaround time with a letter is much slower than with an e-mail. While this is true, there is a difference between writing a letter and pecking off an e-mail, which leads to a second disadvantage of e-mail. E-mail is often written hastily, without much thought going into the message, its organization, sentence structure, grammar, and spelling. If someone is going to take the time to write a letter, he or she will likely have thoughtfully composed it, made sure it was grammatically correct, with all the words spelled correctly.

Another disadvantage with e-mail is that important messages can easily get mixed up with junk e-mail. Also, many senders send their e-mails to so many people that it is sometimes difficult to know exactly to whom the e-mail was really addressed, if a response is requested, who is expected to respond, and whether the response should go just to the sender or to everybody who received it.

Good project managers use e-mail when it is the most effective and appropriate communication tool. They compose their thoughts prior to writing the e-mail. They make their messages concise. They reread them before sending them, making sure that they make sense, are grammatically correct, and that the words are spelled correctly. They use e-mail to:

- Confirm a recent discussion or decision that took place orally between the PM and the receiver. In the e-mail, the PM requests confirmation from the receiver.
- Communicate simple, clear-cut factual information that requires no feedback from the receiver to understand the message.
- Transmit lengthy documents as attachments to the e-mail—reports, drawings, memos, requests for proposals, etc.

Good PMs do not use e-mail:

- in lieu of decision-making and/or brainstorming meetings that require direct interaction and simultaneous participation by many individuals;
- to share important, complicated information that may require follow-up questions before the receiver fully understands the message.

The characteristics needed for managing design projects are a rare combination of skills, experience, and personal character. They are not acquired overnight. They take years of practice and require learning from one's own mistakes and from the mistakes of others. For project managers, there is always something new to learn.

CHAPTER 4 CHECKLIST

Project managers are generalists. Good project managers possess the right combination of personality traits and skills. Project managers should ask:

❐ Do I have a high motivation to manage a design team of intelligent, well-educated, creative people?
❐ Do I behave ethically, honestly, and professionally at all times regardless of the temptations to act otherwise?
❐ Do I have the necessary technical background and state licenses to lead this project?
❐ Am I a pragmatist? Am I willing to make decisions based on achieving particular project outcomes?
❐ Will I use all three inference tools of logic—deduction, induction, and abduction—to assist me in making outcome-oriented decisions?
❐ Am I able and willing to make decisions with incomplete information?

❐ Can I enable—empower—the design team?

❐ Do I have a balanced appreciation for the technical, functional, aesthetic, and financial parameters that affect project decision making?

❐ Can I communicate effectively—orally, in writing, and graphically?

❐ Do I strive for perfection but am willing to accept practical compromises?

❐ Am I able and willing to lead, teach, nurture, and coach others?

C h a p t e r

5

PLANNING THE PROJECT

Most clichés become clichés because they are true. "Failing to plan is planning to fail" was first coined more than 40 years ago by Harvard MBA and time-management consultant Alan Lakein. It was true when he said it, it was probably true before he said it, and it certainly is true in the design professions. It has since passed into that timeless realm of clichés, taking its place alongside that other cliché that applies equally well to planning, "A stitch in time saves nine."

Design professionals are planners by profession. They spend every day planning and designing projects for their clients. They try out various alternatives, making sketches over and over until the design is just right. They try out different structural systems, framing plans, foundation alternatives. They study alternative furniture layouts and color schemes. Yet, they often fail to plan their own work. It is like the story about the cobbler who makes shoes every day for his customers but forgets to make them for his own children.

A design project must be planned. This is the only consistent way of achieving project success without blindly hoping for a lucky roll of the dice. Not planning projects is also a plan, a bad plan. It is a plan to fail.

Design projects are not all the same. A bridge is not a treatment plant, a treatment plant is not a house, and a house is not a 20-story office building. Design projects are not routine endeavors. They require creativity and solving the specific problems of each project. However, most design projects are not breakthrough projects either, with none other like them. Similarities exist among the majority of design projects. All require planning, development of the design, and production of construction documents—plans and specifications. Because there are many similarities among projects, there are similarities in the process of planning the design work.

Once the project is defined (see the activities of project management in Chapter 2), the second task is to plan how to do the project. This requires developing a project work plan. A project work plan is a step-by-step method for accomplishing the work. A project work plan is the process of planning ahead, thinking about what the overall project objectives are, and then defining the incremental steps needed to accomplish them. Figure 5.1 illustrates what can happen when one does not plan ahead before executing a project.

NASA did not get to the moon because the first thing it did was to fire a big rocket. It got to the moon because firing the rocket was among the last things it did. A great deal of planning and thousands of small incremental steps preceded the actual launch. Everyone knows what Neil Armstrong said when he first put his foot on the moon: "One small step for man, one giant leap for mankind." A giant leap, yes, but it was the small steps of a well-thought-out and executed plan that got him there.

Building design is not rocket science. Nevertheless, a building does not design itself. The modern building is a complicated assemblage of materials and systems. It requires a team

FIGURE 5.1 Project Planning

Project planning requires thinking ahead and identifying all the incremental steps needed to accomplish the project.

effort of highly trained and specialized design professionals to pull it off. It requires a plan to organize the design work and the design team.

By now it should be clear: the person responsible for preparing the plan and making sure it is executed properly is the project manager.

KNOW THE TERRITORY

Properly planning design projects requires two kinds of knowledge: knowledge of project management and knowledge that comes from the experience of actually doing design work. A project manager must know both territories.

In the Broadway musical *The Music Man*, the anvil salesman argues that to sell anvils (and presumably musical instruments), "You've got to know the territory." The same can be said for managing design projects. The project manager must know the design profession territory. The project manager must know enough about the nature of the work to properly plan it, manage it, and understand what design team members say and do. The project manager must also know enough about the work to avoid design problems and how to resolve them if they do occur.

The project manager, however, does not have to know all the ins and outs of how to do all the work in detail. Remember from Chapter 4, project managers are generalists. No one person can design all the pieces. Design is a team effort these days, with the project manager in the role of team leader. But the project manager does need to understand the work, at least conceptually. In areas where the project manager feels uncomfortable, unsure, or beyond his or her experience or area of expertise, the project manager must consult with other team members or principals, superiors, or supervisors with the necessary experience.

To reiterate what was said in Chapter 4, the project manager has to determine what he or she knows, what he or she does not know, and when to seek help and from whom. This is essential if the project is to succeed.

For example, this story comes from the construction industry but it applies equally well to design. First the moral of the story: A PM must plan the work and the plan must be based on a sound understanding of the work involved.

A general contractor was constructing a building with a very large basement. The basement walls were formed and the reinforcing steel was in place. The project's superintendent (equivalent to a design project PM) was entrusted with planning the erection of the formwork and the concrete pour for the basement walls. The superintendent decided to construct a steep dirt access ramp down into the hole in the ground that would eventually become the basement. The ramp was the only way down and the only way back out. He positioned the concrete pumper down in the center of the hole with the idea of pumping all the concrete into the basement walls formwork from this one position without having to move the pumper.

On the day of the pour, the first concrete truck arrived and went down the ramp. The concrete pumper began pumping the wet concrete into the forms. Concrete workers up on the form scaffolding moved the hose along the forms. Others vibrated the concrete down into the forms to make sure that the concrete properly filled in around the reinforcing steel so there would not be any voids. As the pumper was pumping the first truck dry, the second truck arrived and waited at the top of the hole. When the truck in the hole was empty, it started back up the ramp. But the dirt ramp was too steep. The truck got stuck. The more the driver gunned the engine, the faster the wheels spun and the deeper the truck sank into the ramp. The ramp was not wide enough for the second truck to pass by the truck that was stuck. So the driver of the second truck waited impatiently at the top of the hole.

Meanwhile, another concrete truck arrived, then another and another. By the time the first truck finally made its way out of the hole, the concrete in the waiting trucks was beginning to stiffen up. Concrete workers call it "getting hot" because concrete heats up when it is setting. Adding water to the mix, "cooling it down," would have made the concrete flow better, but it also would have reduced the strength of the concrete. This was unacceptable from an engineering point of view. Sending the trucks away would have meant wasting the concrete, but, more important to the superintendent, all the money spent to buy the concrete would be wasted, too. Concrete batch plants do not give refunds or take back unused wet concrete because wet concrete doesn't stay wet for long.

So the superintendent decided to pour anyway. He did it as quickly as possible, pumping one truck right after the other at a frantic pace. In their haste, the concrete workers let the concrete free-fall into the forms. This caused the water, cement, and aggregate in the concrete to separate as the concrete fell, splashing and bouncing off of formwork and reinforcing steel. Also, the concrete was not properly vibrated to make sure it worked its way around the reinforcing steel.

When the forms were stripped many days later, the ugly truth was revealed. There were numerous rock pockets and voids in the wall and around the reinforcing steel. The owner was terribly upset and worried. There was a meeting—a big, big meeting. The superintendent and the owner of the contracting company listened for a couple of hours to complaints, questions, and second guessing. Why was there only one ramp? Didn't the contractor know it was too steep? Why was there only one pumper and why was it positioned in the hole? Why did the contractor pour concrete that was starting to set up? Why did the contractor let the concrete free-fall into the forms and why wasn't it vibrated? The superintendent did not have good answers. Eventually, the superintendent admitted that this was the largest pour he had ever undertaken and that he had not asked anyone for help in planning the concrete pour. The contractor spent the next three months fixing the mistake, a mistake that could have been avoided had a work plan been developed based on sound practical experience.

This example shows what can go wrong if the person doing the planning does not possess the necessary expertise and fails to consult with someone who does. In addition, it illustrates how a poor work plan can be made worse if additional poor decisions are made.

A good project manager has to know the job, that is the territory. The project manager has to understand the work well enough to plan it properly and be wise enough to know when to seek advice. When the project manager does not know a certain aspect of the work—and this is both understandable and common—the project manager must consult with others who do.

ITERATIVE PROJECT PLANNING

Planning a project is an iterative process—like drawing a cartoon. Suppose a cartoonist wants to draw a cartoon of someone running. The cartoonist does not start with the cartoon character's shoe and draw it in complete detail and then, when finished with the shoe, move on to the trousers, then the torso, head, etc. The cartoonist starts with the whole character, sketching it loosely, diagrammatically, without any detail, to establish its basic size, shape, and the relationship of its component parts. Once the cartoonist is satisfied with the overall size, shape, and composition, more detail is added. When satisfied with this, the cartoonist then adds even more details until the cartoon is complete. The process is iterative, worked on in multiple attempts or passes, with each pass adding additional details. Figure 5.2 illustrates this iterative approach.

The actual design process—the third phase of the five project phases—is also iterative. Consequently, it should be relatively easy for design professionals to grasp the concept and importance of iterative project planning. In design, the big picture is developed first—conceptually, without much detail. Once the big picture is conceptually completed, more detail is added as the design develops.

Before beginning the project planning process, the project manager must read and understand the contract or agreement between the owner and the design professional. Often the agreement breaks down the project into parts or phases, with specific submission requirements—often called deliverables—at

FIGURE 5.2 Iterative Process

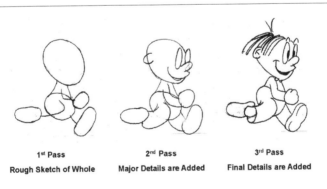

| 1st Pass | 2nd Pass | 3rd Pass |
| Rough Sketch of Whole | Major Details are Added | Final Details are Added |

THE ITERATIVE PROCESS

The cartoonist is like the project planner. The cartoonist starts with the basics in a rough-sketch form. With each pass more detail is added until the cartoon is finished.

the end of each phase. For example, "schematic," "design development," and "construction document" phases are common terms used in owner/design professional agreements. Using the same terms that the agreement uses, the project is first divided into its major phases. Each phase is then further broken down into its major tasks. After that, the major tasks are broken down into subtasks. Figure 5.3 illustrates this iterative process.

FIGURE 5.3   Project Planning Is Iterative

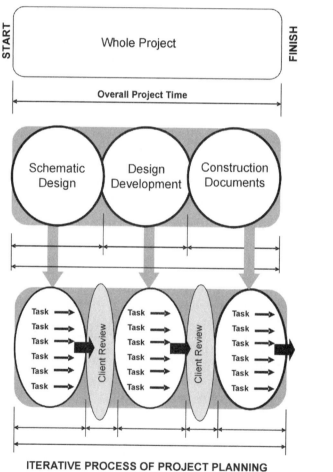

ITERATIVE PROCESS OF PROJECT PLANNING

The project planner starts with the whole project in rough form. With each planning iteration more details are added until the project work plan is finished.

Another way of thinking about the project is to think about it as a series of aerial photographs. The first picture is taken high overhead, for example, at the 10,000-foot level. It is an overview that shows everything, but nothing in detail. Another picture is taken at a lower altitude where major characteristics of the project terrain are discernible. Finally, a series of pictures are taken, hovering directly over different parts of the project, showing every part of the project in fine detail.

Whichever comparison one prefers—the cartoon or the aerial photograph analogy—the point is the same. Planning starts with the all-inclusive big view and then focuses in on the project in more and more detail through a series of passes.

While planning and design work are done iteratively, project production and task work are not. They are done linearly, one bite at a time (see Figure 5.4).

Parents everywhere tell their children to clean their plates. They instruct them to take small bites, chew each piece, and swallow it before taking the next bite. Good advice. In fact, it

FIGURE 5.4 Project Planning and Design

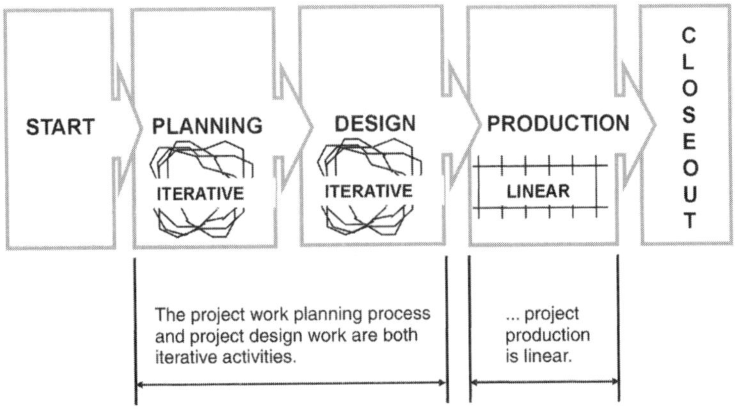

Planning the project and designing the project are iterative activities. Project production—the making of contract documents or contract deliverables—is linear.

is such sage wisdom that, given enough time, one could eat an entire whale following this plan.

Planning large projects is a lot like eating a whale. The trick is to divide the project into manageable bites or pieces—called tasks—and then chew them in the correct order (see Figure 5.5). Of course, unlike whale eating, the purpose of planning a design project is not to clean one's plate. It is to accomplish the project objectives and to meet all the project management goals.

A fish-bone diagram is a useful tool for whale eating, that is, for planning a project. A fish-bone diagram is so-named because—with a bit of imagination—it resembles the skeleton of a fish. (Yes, I am using mixed metaphors and I do realize that a whale is not a fish!)

The fish-bone diagram was first developed in Japan by Dr. Kaoru Ishikawa (1915–1989). It is a graphic way of dividing a project, or problem, into its cause-and-effect bites (see Figure 5.6). It diagrams all the inputs to an output according to their relationship to each other and by their level of importance or detail. Dr. Ishikawa used the fish-bone diagram to graphically show and analyze the many factors that could be causing a production problem that he wanted to solve. Using the fish-bone diagram in reverse, it can be used to plan a project by diagramming all the cause-and-effect tasks that are necessary to complete a project.

FIGURE 5.5   Eating a Whale

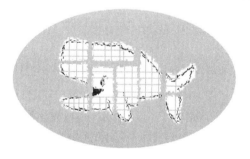

Planning a large project is like eating a whale. The trick is to divide it up into manageable bites.

FIGURE 5.6 Fish-Bone Diagram

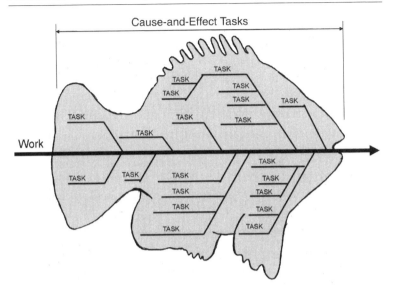

A fish-bone diagram shows the cause-and-effect tasks that must be performed to successfully complete a project.

In school, almost everyone learned how to diagram a sentence by breaking it down into its word parts. The sentence diagram graphically showed how the subject, verb, object, adjectives, adverbs, and prepositions related to one another and to the sentence as a whole. Figure 5.7 illustrates a sentence diagram.

FIGURE 5.7 Sentence Diagram

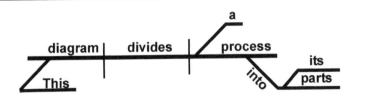

This diagram divides a process into its parts.

A sentence diagram shows how the different parts of a sentence relate to one another and to the whole sentence.

A fish-bone diagram does the same thing for large projects. Instead of words, however, it shows tasks and illustrates their interdependencies and relationships to the whole project.

The overall objective of a design project is to produce the design or provide the services as described and required by the agreement between the design firm and the client. In effect, the agreement defines—at least in very general terms—the project's scope of work.

The purpose of a project work plan is to flesh out the scope of work as defined in the agreement and to clarify it in enough detail so that a team of design professionals can effectively work on it. The project work plan also divides the project into logical tasks for performance and monitoring purposes. In addition, it establishes team member responsibilities, the project's reporting structure, and project-specific procedures, such as safety procedures, Computer Aided Design and Drafting (CADD) standards, and quality-control procedures. It provides necessary information to the design firm's accounting department so project job costs can be properly categorized and invoiced. Finally, it provides project information to the firm's upper management so it has confidence that the project has been properly planned.

Not making a work plan is risky. The project objectives may not be clear to the design team members. If the objectives are not clear, the tasks required to accomplish the project cannot be clear, either. If a project starts without a plan, some task work may be wasted because it was not necessary to perform in the first place. Other tasks may be left out. Even if the objectives are known, it is difficult to focus clearly on them if the work is done in a hodgepodge fashion rather than in the logical sequence that a well-thought-out plan provides. Without a work plan, it is easy to make mistakes.

SIX OBJECTIVES OF THE PROJECT WORK PLAN

There are six objectives of the project work plan. These are:

1. Definition of the project objectives
2. Identification of the project team
3. Breakdown of the project into task budgets
4. Development of the project schedule
5. Establishment of the project quality-control program
6. Identification of other project-specific procedures and standards

Items 3, 4, and 5 —project task budgets, schedule, and quality control—will only be touched on in this chapter but discussed in more detail in Chapters 7, 9, and 12, respectively.

Definition of the Project Objectives

Before a journalist begins writing a news story, he or she asks the questions: who, what, why, where, when, and how? This is just about the first thing a student learns in journalism school. The answers to these questions help the journalist write the story and stay focused on the objectives of the story.

Before beginning the project, the project manager should ask similar questions. The answers to the questions will help to define the project's overall objectives. The project manager's questions are only slightly different from the journalist's.

To understand the project objectives, the questions the project manager should ask before beginning a project are: what, when, who, and how much? Expanded, the questions become:

- What is to be done?
- When is it to be done?
- Who is to do it?
- How much will it cost to do it?

The important words are *do* and *done*. They imply an action, doing something. Doing something produces an outcome. Outcomes can be measured. Project objectives and the goals of project management are measurable.

For example, suppose a design firm has a contract to design an office building for the EFG Corporation with a total area of 100,000 square feet. The design fee is $1.9 million. Attached to the contract are three exhibits. Exhibit A contains the project schedule that shows a design period of 14 months. Exhibit B is a program of spaces that defines the number, sizes, and functions of the spaces (rooms) required. Exhibit C includes a budget of $27 million for the construction of the project.

The contract also contains information about insurance requirements, billing procedures, etc. The project manager must read and understand all of this, but for the purpose of defining the project objectives, the project manager must sift through the contract and extract the information needed to answer the four questions: what, when, who, and how? For the EFG Building, the project objectives are:

- What? Design and prepare construction documents for a $27 million, 100,000-square-foot office building based on the program of spaces as contained in Exhibit B. This summarizes the project objectives. It also establishes the construction cost portion of the baseline for meeting the project management goal of finishing the project within budget—a building design that can be built for $27 million. (Recall the project management goals from Chapter 2.)
- When? The design and construction documents must be completed and ready for bid in 14 months. This establishes the design-work portion of the baseline for meeting the project management goal of finishing the project on schedule.
- Who? The design firm will do the project. (Sometimes design firms must hire consultants to perform some of the

work and sometimes the client provides certain information: survey and/or geotechnical report, for example.)

- How much? The project budget is $1.9 million, equal to the design fee. This establishes the design portion of the baseline for meeting the project management goal of finishing the project within budget.

These are the broad-brush overall project objectives and, as shown, set the baselines for many of the project management goals. The object is not just to design the building. That is a gross generalization and consequently misleading. The design firm will not be happy if it takes $2.5 million to design the project. Accomplishing the work within budget is definitely an important goal to the design firm.

Meeting the schedule is necessary, too. The client is not likely to be pleased if it takes 24 months instead of 14 months to complete the design. Remember that all four questions must be asked and answered.

Note that the answers to the four questions are concise and measurable. As the project work plan develops in more detail, additional project objectives will be fleshed out and these, too, require clear measurable outcomes.

The answer to the "How much?" question will vary from office to office. The answer given previously may actually be incorrect for some design offices. True, the design fee is $1.9 million, but that does not necessarily mean that this is how much money the project manager has to do the project. Depending on the design firm's project accounting procedures, this number may require some adjusting. Some design firms build profit into their hourly rates and hourly cost-accounting practices while others do not. If the design firm keeps track of profit separately and sets a goal that it would like to achieve a profit of perhaps 8 percent for all its projects, then the total $1.9 million is not available to the project manager; only $1.75 million is available ($1.9 million × 0.92). This $150,000 is profit that the project manager had better not spend.

The project manager may not want to budget the project work to spend all the money available. It might be a good idea to set aside some money as a contingency and plan to complete all the project tasks without spending the contingency. Design projects are not immune from Murphy's Law, as Arthur Bloch so wittily and succinctly stated in his 1977 book of the same name—"If anything can go wrong, it will" and "Everything takes longer than you think it will."[36] Something unexpected almost always happens on projects. Consequently, it is a good idea to squirrel away a little money for the unexpected. By the way, I know a few project managers who use the task name "Acorns" to represent their projects' contingency funds.

The following story illustrates how the unexpected can happen at any time and the importance of having a contingency fund. I recall losing the lead in-house civil engineer from one of my projects without the civil engineer ever quitting. In the middle of preparing working drawings, the office manager reassigned the civil engineer to another project because Murphy had reared his ugly head on that other project and more help was needed to meet its deadline. This left my project without a civil engineer. I scrambled and found another. But the replacement civil engineer and I had to spend quite a few hours together—meaning dollars—bringing her up to speed on the project. Fortunately, I had acorns squirreled away.

How much should be squirreled away is a judgment call that varies from project to project, depending on the complexity, size, and number of disciplines working on the project. A contingency of 10 percent is a very common percentage, but other percentages may make more sense taking into account project specifics.

Identification of the Project Team

The answer to the "Who is to do it?" question needs further definition. While the answer, "The design firm does the work," is contractually correct, it is too general to serve the needs of the project manager and the design team members who will perform the work. It begs further questions about what disciplines are needed: architecture, structural, mechanical, etc.? Who are the key individuals within each discipline who will do the work? Will all the disciplines and team members be in-house or will outside consultants be needed to perform some of the work? Who is responsible for whom and what are the responsibilities of the various team members? These questions require answers. The answers to these questions will help the project manager assemble a design team with the appropriate skills needed to perform the work.

Once the project manager has selected the project team, the team and the relationships of the team members can be neatly summarized in a project organization chart. The project organization chart graphically shows the disciplines required to do the work and the reporting structure for the project. The chart can also show which disciplines are in-house and which are consultants. It should include the names and project titles of the key team members. It should always include the quality-assurance/quality-control manager (QA/QC manager), the project principal, and the CADD manager. It should include the project controller, if there is one. Figure 5.8 shows a typical organizational chart for a multidisciplinary design project.

Sometimes project roles are complicated and cannot be reduced to just a word or two on a project organizational chart. In these cases, written descriptions of key team members' roles and responsibilities are very helpful. All project team members need to know what is expected of them. Important information and/or tasks can fall through the cracks if they do not. It must be clear to everyone what they are expected to do.

All work requires somebody to do it. Work does not do itself. This sounds so obvious that it may not seem worth mentioning, but it is. Sometimes minor, but necessary, project work is not assigned and sometimes this minor work requires expertise not found among any of the team members.

FIGURE 5.8   A Typical Organization Chart for a Multidisciplinary Design Project

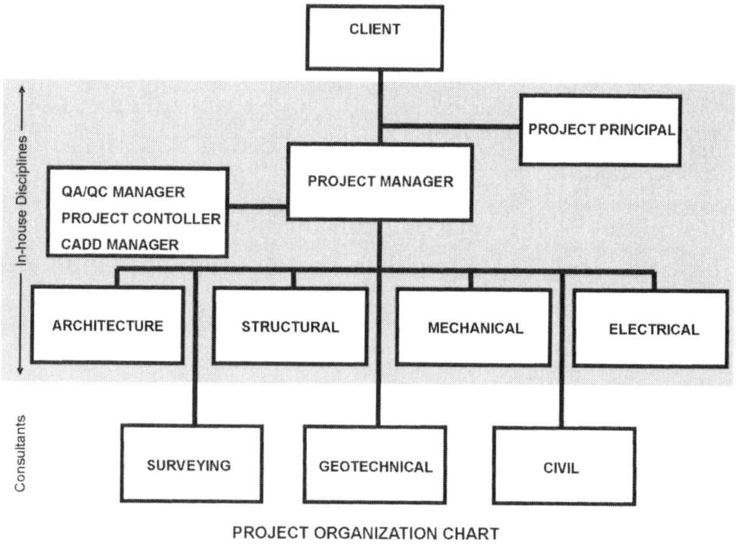

PROJECT ORGANIZATION CHART

For example, very few interior remodeling projects require civil engineering, but occasionally some do. Perhaps a new utility connection or upgrade of an existing utility is needed. Maybe a new handicap-accessible curb cut is required. If the project manager fails to include a civil engineer on such a project's design team, it is pretty much a certainty nobody will design and detail the utility connection, or service upgrade, or the handicap curb cut. It is important to include all the disciplines needed to complete all the required tasks, no matter how small.

It is also helpful to get buy-in from team members and their supervisors. It is best to solicit their input when developing the work plan. Chapter 10 describes a useful tool for this called the wall chart. Everybody likes to know about and participate in determining their future. Team members will be happier if they are asked first, not told later. Also, they may not be available for some reason and it is better to know that sooner rather than later.

If it is not practical or possible to get potential team members involved from the beginning, then at a minimum get their review as a courtesy and get their commitment to the project before finalizing the project team. Make sure all team members will be available when the time comes for them to do the project work.

The organization chart in Figure 5.9 shows the project roles of CADD manager, QA/QC manager, and project controller. These roles require an explanation.

Project CADD Manager. The design professions underwent a profound change during the late 1980s and early 1990s. Within a period of less than ten years, design professionals stopped drawing by hand and began drawing with a computer. Contract drawings are now generated using computer-aided design and drafting (CADD) programs. There are a few different CADD programs, but basically one of two software programs dominate the industry, AutoCAD and MicroStation. Of the two, AutoCAD is far more prevalent.

FIGURE 5.9 Project Responsibilities

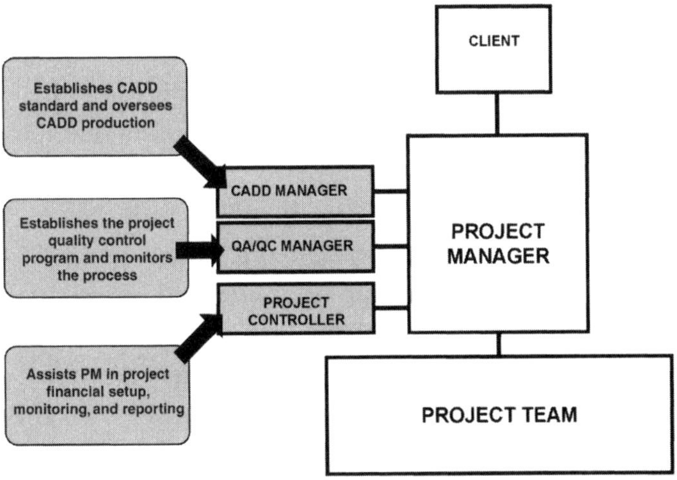

The responsibilities of the project CADD manager, QA/QC manager, and the project controller.

On multidisciplinary design projects, CADD drafters/designers of various disciplines must use and share common computer drawing files. Consequently, the drawing files and procedures must be standardized. The CADD manager must set standards and make sure that all the disciplines follow them. Filename and layering conventions, pen-color, and line-plotting requirements must be determined and used consistently from discipline to discipline. Drafting standards such as style and size of text, cross-referencing standards, symbols, and dimensioning standards (arrows versus ticks, curved leaders versus straight-line leaders) must be determined, along with many other drawing standards. The purpose is to provide the basic framework within which all the drawings are produced, regardless of discipline, so that they can be easily used as reference backgrounds (Xrefs) by other disciplines and to give the drawings a consistent and coordinated look when plotted.

Many clients have their own drafting standards that must be followed. The CADD manager must make sure that all the team members are aware of the client's standards, that they understand how the client's standards may vary from the firm's standards, and to spot-check drawings to see that the client's standards are followed.

Drawings produced by multiple offices and drawings produced by consultants pose special communication challenges for the CADD manager. All offices and consultants must understand and follow the standards.

Project QA/QC Manager. Clients expect projects to be error-free. From a practical point of view, this is impossible. It is possible, however, to establish procedures for quality control and to assign someone to oversee the quality-control program so that mistakes are kept to a minimum. This person is the quality-assurance/quality-control or QA/QC manager. Because quality is so important for design firms, Chapter 12 will cover a project quality-control program in more detail.

Project Controller. Before computers were introduced, keeping track of a project's finances was hit-and-miss. Some project managers had their own ways of keeping track of their projects' financials. Others hardly kept track at all. More and more firms are using integrated software programs that combine time cards, payroll, business development, accounts payable and receivable, and project management. Using these programs is often less than intuitive. Many programs require special expertise to understand and use them. Training is required and constant use is necessary to remember how to use all the features and to make the programs do what one wants them to do.

Many firms provide periodic financial reports and/or have project-review requirements. It can take considerable time to prepare the paperwork needed to keep upper management informed, time that many project managers do not have, particularly if the computer software program the firm uses is complicated and requires special expertise to master. This is where the project controller comes in. The project controller's role is to keep the project manager out of financial reporting trouble with upper management and to help the project manager see potential financial problems coming along well enough in advance so the project manager has enough time to take corrective measures. Some firms assign every project a project controller.

Breakdown of the Project into Task Budgets

Children are often told to do their chores. The word *chores*, however, has no specific meaning. At some point, Mom or Dad have to define the chores. "Johnny, every Saturday morning you must mow the lawn." "Take out the kitchen garbage every night after dinner." "Clean the birdcage Wednesdays after school." These are defined chores. They have defined scopes of work that are easy to understand. Johnny knows what he is supposed to do and Mom or Dad can easily tell whether he has done his chores or not. "Do your homework" is not a well-defined chore because Mom or Dad can not really tell if all the homework is done independently from Johnny saying that it is.

In project management parlance, defined chores are called *tasks*. Remember Taylor's breakdown of work into tasks as discussed in Chapter 1. A task is an essential activity or increment of work. Every task requires three elements to fully define it.

1. An objective
2. A duration
3. A level of effort

The *objective* must have a measurable outcome, a way of knowing whether it is completed or not. The *duration* is the length of time budgeted to reach the objective. For most projects, time duration is measured in workdays or calendar days. The *level of effort* is generally measured in hours and is the number of labor hours budgeted to accomplish the objective. The level of effort can also be measured in labor dollars.

An item of work that does not include all three elements is not a task. For example, if the project manager assigns Joan the responsibility of preparing the door schedule and detailing all the doors, has Joan been given a task? No. Joan has an assignment, an activity with an objective but no duration or level of effort associated with it. How does Joan know how many days she has to complete the assignment? How does Joan know if she has 20 hours, 30 hours, or even 400 hours to spend doing the assignment? The answer is: she does not. Almost certainly, if an activity is assigned without a time duration and an effort budget, it will take too long and too many hours to complete. The PM must make sure all assignments or activities are really tasks, with an associated objective, duration, and level of effort.

Structuring the Tasks. When most design professionals hear the word *structure,* they think of a bridge or a dam or the skeleton-like structural system for a building. But the word *structure* can be used in other ways. For example, the iterative planning process described previously has a definite structure to it. It is a stable, consistent, and repeatable process that can be used on project after project. The term *structure* can be used to describe any system that is relatively fixed, repeatable, and composed of interrelated parts that form the whole.

Identifying and defining all the necessary project tasks is a major step. But arranging them in a meaningful, structured way makes them into a useful tool. The common structure used to organize project tasks into a useful form is called the work breakdown structure (WBS). Remember the discussion of work breakdown structures in Chapter 1.

A good WBS includes the following characteristics:

- It is developed iteratively, starting with the whole and getting more and more detailed with each subsequent pass.
- It is hierarchical, that is, component parts relate to each other in terms of importance.
- It has the right amount of detail, no more and certainly no less.
- Tasks are defined by objective, duration, and level of effort.
- It is based on relevant past experience in both project management and design.

Work breakdown structures can take the form of lists or tree structures. In general, the tree-structure approach better illustrates how the tasks relate to each other. Most design firms' project accounting systems, however, cannot deal with the graphic nature of the tree structure so the list format is the more commonly used of the two.

The list format, however, often leads to overlisting. Projects become grocery lists of activities, which frequently leads project managers to micromanage projects. This makes project management time consuming and difficult to manage, monitor, and judge progress. Remember, tasks have objectives, durations, and levels of effort. Grocery lists are just that, lists of activities with little or no accountability.

If it is set up correctly, the work breakdown structure is a helpful project planning tool. It is also used to judge a project's performance, allowing the project manager to compare progress against budgets. Chapter 8 looks at the WBS in more detail.

Development of the Project Schedule

The purpose of project scheduling is to determine how to perform the work so that it can be completed on time. It tells team members when information and deliverables are due throughout the course of the project. The project manager also uses the project schedule as a timeline benchmark, against which project progress can be compared to see if work is being accomplished at the pace it should be. Chapter 9 discusses project scheduling in more detail.

Establishment of the Project Quality-Control Program

The purpose of the project quality-control program is to establish the quality-control procedures for the project. Project work must be as complete and accurate as possible, meaning the project must address and satisfy all the client's objectives. Project management goals and all project deliverables must be as error-free as possible. The project work plan should identify the project's quality-control manager and explain the project quality-control procedures that are to be followed. The procedures may be the firm's standard procedures or they may be special procedures as required by the client through the agreement. Chapter 11 discusses project quality control.

Identification of Other Project-Specific Procedures and Standards

Other procedures and standards should be addressed when developing the project work plan. These include such things as a project work safety plan, CADD and drafting standards, special project accounting and invoicing procedures, project filing standards, and standard formats for documenting telephone calls and project meetings.

Project Work Safety Plan. Performing project work safely is one of the six goals of project management. If the project includes field visits and/or various site investigations, the project work plan should address safety procedures. Many clients need advance notice if members of the team are going to show up on-site. If so, design team members need to know this. Some clients have special safety procedures that must be followed. For example, the client may require using hard hats, safety shoes, goggles, and/or ear protection. If so, this information must be communicated to the design team. If hazardous materials are on the site, team members must be warned and told (or reminded) of the procedures to follow.

Project CADD and Drafting Standards. The project work plan should identify the project CADD manager and explain his or her responsibilities. The plan should identify the CADD procedures and drafting standards that are to be followed. Many design firms follow their own CADD standards and some have their CADD standards formalized into manuals. Some clients set their own standards, however, and many require that their standards be followed. If so, the project manager must communicate this to the design team. Failure to do so could result in a lot of CADD drawing cleanup and rework to get the drawings into the format requested by the client.

Project Filing Standards. An important part of every project is keeping track of the paperwork. The project work plan should establish both the computer and hard-copy filing standards. Large projects may require a project clerk to assist the PM with filing and keeping track of documents. Many large design firms have standardized filing systems, but some are so flexible that they require the PM to determine the specific files needed for a particular project.

Phone Conversations and Memorandums. The project work plan should establish specific formats for documenting phone conversations and meetings. As with filing systems, many firms use standard forms for telephone memos and meeting minutes.

THE PROJECT WORK PLAN DOCUMENT

Once the plan for doing the work is figured out, it should be committed to paper. The project work plan document provides the basic project information and describes the planning activities and procedures necessary for the team members to effectively do their work. Following is a suggested format for the project work plan document. In addition, this serves as a good checklist for developing a comprehensive project work plan.

Outline of a Typical Project Work Plan Document

1. Project objectives
   - General description of the project, including any unusual project features
   - Major project objectives
   - Major milestones (project phases)
   - Project construction budget, if known
   - Deliverables by milestones or phases (often takes the form of lists of drawings, specifications, reports, etc.; required at the end of each phase)

2. Project team
   - Project organization chart
   - List of key team members, names, affiliations (in-house or consultants), phone numbers, and addresses
   - Roles and responsibilities of key team members
3. Project task-budget information
   - List of project tasks and their budgets (expressed as dollars or hours)
   - WBS task codes (time-card charge codes)
   - ODC (other direct cost) budgets (expressed as dollars)
4. Project schedule information
   - Project schedule
   - Project milestone information
5. Project quality-control procedures
   - Quality-control plan
   - Identification of quality-control manager
   - Quality-control procedures
6. Miscellaneous procedures
   - Accounting/invoicing information
   - Project safety procedures
   - CADD and drafting standards and procedures, including identification of CADD manager
   - Project filing procedures
   - Telephone conversation and meeting minutes standard formats

The order of the information contained in the project work plan document is not so important as making sure it includes all the pertinent information: everything the project team needs to do its job; everything the accounting department needs to invoice the job; the information upper management needs to feel confident that the project manager has a workable plan for running the job; and everything the PM needs to properly lead, manage, and monitor the project.

The project work plan document should be distributed to all team members, the accounting department, and to appropriate firm management personnel, which may include the project manager's supervisor, the firm's quality-control officer, and principal(s).

Generally, it is not necessary to give a copy to the client. The project work plan is intended to be an internal communications document. The client may have requested parts of it, however, through the agreement. For example, the project schedule and the quality-control program are often requested by clients.

After distribution, it is often a good idea to follow up with a team meeting to go over the project work plan. The team members will have had a chance to see and digest the information before the meeting. They may have questions, comments, and/or concerns. These can be addressed during the meeting. If something significant changes because of the meeting, then a revised project work plan document should be distributed.

As the project moves along, things may change. Items may be added to the scope of work by the client. The schedules might change. New information and changed conditions must be distributed to the project team. If the project work plan is not updated, sooner or later it becomes seriously out-of-date. If too many things have changed and the plan is not updated, team members will stop looking at it for guidance. Good project managers keep their project work plans up-to-date.

CHAPTER 5 CHECKLIST

Because "Failing to plan is planning to fail," a project work plan should be developed before beginning every project. The person responsible for developing the work plan is the PM. Two kinds of knowledge are required to properly plan a project:

1. An understanding of project management
2. The technical knowledge and experience that comes from actually doing design work

The project planning process is iterative, while production task work is linear.

There are six objectives of the project work plan. These are:

1. Definition of the project objectives
2. Identification of the project team
3. Breakdown of the project into task budgets
4. Development of the project schedule
5. Establishment of the project quality-control program
6. Identification of other project-specific procedures and standards

Before beginning the project work plan, the PM should ask the following questions:

❑ Did I read and do I understand the project contract?
❑ Are the project objectives defined? Were the questions "What, when, who, and how much?" answered?
❑ Are the major parts or phases of the project defined?
❑ Do I have the right design team?
❑ Did I create a project team organization chart and are all the key team members and disciplines identified?
❑ Are the key work tasks identified?
❑ Does every task have an objective, duration, and budget effort?
❑ Did I create a project work plan to document all the project requirements?
❑ Does the project work plan address the following: project objectives, project team organization, project budget and accounting information, project schedule, quality-control procedures, safety procedures, CADD standards, and project filing system?
❑ Did I give the project work plan to all the team members?
❑ If the work plan changed during the course of the work, did I update the plan and redistribute it to all the key team members?

THE NEXT CHAPTER

Properly planning the project greatly increases its chances of success. Said another way, proper planning greatly reduces the project's risk.

Risk is the possibility that something will go wrong with the project. Project managers must manage risk and keep it to a minimum. The next chapter explores various ways of managing project risk.

C h a p t e r

6

PROJECT RISK MANAGEMENT

Design projects are inherently risky. Every project is different in some way and this carries with it uncertainties. In project management parlance, *risk* is the term used to describe the amount of uncertainty and number of threats (elements that threaten the success of the project) that exist or potentially exist in a project. The greater the amount of uncertainty and number of threats, the greater the risk (see Figure 6.1).

While it is not possible to alleviate all risks, some risks can be eliminated by thoughtful problem solving, while others can be successfully managed so their impact on the project is kept to a minimum.

When the coach of a football team relays the play to the quarterback and the quarterback calls the play in the huddle, a number of uncertainties exist. Will the play work? Will the center-quarterback exchange go smoothly? Will everyone block the way they are supposed to? Will the receiver get open? Will the quarterback throw the ball accurately? Will the receiver catch the ball? Will the pass receiver get tackled and fumble? Will the receiver or someone else on the team get hurt? There are many uncertainties.

FIGURE 6.1   Uncertainty and Risk

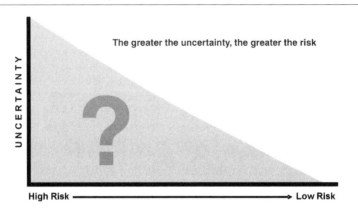

The greater the uncertainty, the greater the risk

UNCERTAINTY

High Risk ⟶ Low Risk

Risk is a measure of the amount of uncertainty and number of threats that can adversely affect a project.

And there are many threats, too. The defensive team might blitz. A linebacker might anticipate a pass, fall back and play pass defense. A defensive back might intercept the football. A pass rusher might evade a blocker, tackle the quarterback, and fall on top of him. The quarterback might end up flat on his back, injured.

To increase the likelihood of the football team winning, the team is, first of all, composed of talented players and coaches who then plan and practice in advance. Every team member knows his role and responsibilities to the team. Plays are practiced over and over. Various scenarios are rehearsed: if this happens, then do this; if that happens, then do that. In football, talented players and coaches who plan and practice are the keys to winning because they reduce the risks that prevent winning.

Design teams, of course, do not have coaches. They have project managers. The project manager must build and lead the project team to success and manage project risk.

Bridge designer Joseph Baerman Strauss (1870–1938) dreamed of designing a structure that could span the San Francisco Golden Gate, the two-mile-wide strait that separates the San Francisco Bay from the Pacific Ocean. Determined that it could be done, he did not listen to the naysayers who said that the idea was preposterous because of the many seemingly insurmountable uncertainties, or risks, associated with such a daunting undertaking. Instead, Strauss went forward with his vision and designed the Golden Gate Bridge (see Figure 6.2) methodically reasoning out solutions to the many design, construction, and nontechnical risks—uncertainties and threats—associated with the project. Stephen Cassady in *Spanning the Gate: The Golden Gate Bridge* wrote:

> Indeed, the man to bridge the Golden Gate could not have been an ordinary civil engineer. The task demanded a visionary . . . a technician . . . an evangelist . . . a politician and a pillar of psychological strength who could remain motivated through fifteen years of obstacles which would have driven a lesser human to lunacy, or at the very least to failure.[37]

STRATEGIES FOR CONTROLLING RISK

PMs must control the threats and uncertainties that could potentially adversely affect their projects. There are a number of strategies for doing this. They include:

- *Prevention*—reduce the number of uncertainties and/or threats
- *Transference*—make some other party responsible for the uncertainties or threats
- *Mitigation*—lessen the impact of the uncertainties or threats should they occur
- *Contingency planning*—plan in advance for coping with uncertainties or threats should they happen
- *Assumption*—identify the uncertainties or threats and accept their potential impact on the project because the cost of prevention, mitigation, transference, and contingency planning are greater than their possible impact

FIGURE 6.2   Golden Gate Bridge

Bridge designer Joseph Strauss successfully managed the design, construction, financial, and political risks that threatened the completion of the Golden Gate Bridge. Photograph by the author.

These strategies are implemented through a variety of risk-management procedures. The obvious ones include:

- Accept only project types with which the firm has a proven and positive track record.
- Work only for past clients where the relationship was successful and avoid working with new clients.
- Use the same design team(s) on all projects because the team has proven it can work together successfully.

These strategies, however, can lead to a stilted practice that becomes so risk-free that it becomes bland, uninteresting, and unchallenging. Most design firms and design professionals want or need challenges. Challenging projects stretch the portfolio of design firms, design professionals, and PMs. Many design firms actively seek out projects that present greater and more rewarding challenges. Many design professionals and PMs seek out design firms with just that attitude.

Of course, new, interesting, and challenging projects present risks. Risks directly associated with the design itself can only be alleviated by good design. The PM and design team should produce the very best design possible to meet the client's and project's needs. But there are other risks design professionals face as well. Surprisingly, many of them are related to the agreement between the owner and the design professional. Design is a challenging and risky enough endeavor as it is without being compounded by natty contractual risks. Fortunately, these can be controlled by employing a few basic risk-management strategies, such as:

1. Use standardized contract forms whenever possible.
2. Understand the provisions of the contract.
3. Avoid contract language that increases risk.
4. Avoid unacceptable risks.
5. Use fee types appropriate for services provided.
6. Provide more comprehensive services.
7. Identify excluded as well as included services.
8. Specify how disputes will be resolved.

Additional, noncontract-related strategies also reduce risk. They are:

9. Inform the client of potential risks.
10. Choose consultants carefully.
11. Do not start production of contract documents until the design is well defined and approved by the client.
12. Avoid running projects without budget and schedule contingencies.

Use Standardized Contract Forms Whenever Possible

The most widely used owner/design professional standardized contracts used for procuring design services are the Standard Form of Agreement Between Owner and Architect (B141), published by the American Institute of Architects (AIA), and the Standard Form of Agreement Between Owner and Engineer for Professional Services (EJCDC 1910-1), published by the Engineers Joint Contract Documents Committee (EJCDC). The EJCDC is composed of members representing the American Society of Civil Engineers (ASCE), the American Consulting Engineers Council (ACEC), and the National Society of Professional Engineers (NSPE).

The AIA has been publishing its owner/architect agreement for more than 100 years and the EJCDC its owner/engineer agreement for more than 30. There are no agreements for design services with greater precedence or wider use than these two. Both are written fairly, without undue prejudice toward or against one party of the contract or the other. They properly define the design services required and the rights and responsibilities of both the owner and the design professional. They have been tested in various court cases and they are updated periodically by their sponsors. They are designed to be easily modified to fit particular project circumstances or owner needs.

Other professional organizations use standardized agreements as well. For example, the Council of American Structural Engineers (CASE) has a standard contract form, Prime Contract, An Agreement Between Owner and Structural Engineer for Professional Services (CASE #13). The Design Build Institute of American (DBIA) publishes a number of model agreements between the owner and design builder that address different contracting arrangements: Preliminary Agreement (DBIA #520), Lump Sum Agreement (DBIA #525), and Cost Plus Fee With or Without a Guaranteed Maximum Price (DBIA #530). The American Society of Foundation Engineers (ASFE) and the American Society of Landscape Architects (ASLA) make various sample contracts available to their members.

Using the AIA's or the EJCDC's or one of the other professional organizations' standard documents is sound professional practice. It is important to tailor the agreements to meet specific project and client needs. Doing so will alleviate many project uncertainties and consequently reduce project risk. Do not reinvent the wheel (see Rule of Thumb 5 in Chapter 13 for more about the problems of reinventing). It is worth remembering that design professionals are not lawyers. So take advantage of the expertise and legal precedents that are available.

Understand the Provisions of the Contract

Some design firms have developed their own standard agreements. Generally, these are based on the AIA's, the EJCDC's, or one of the other professional organizations' agreements in combination with the firm's own past experiences. In such cases, the project manager should read, understand, and use the firm's standard agreement and then customize it for a project's specific needs.

Many owners have their own agreement forms, too. Usually such agreements favor the owner. Sometimes these agreements treat design services much like the owner was procuring equipment, products, supplies, or contracting services. Indeed, some refer to the design professional as the "contractor" within the agreement. Some owners claim that their agreements are not negotiable, maintaining that if the design firm wants the work it must accept the agreement as is. Usually, however, owners are willing to negotiate, at least a bit.

The project manager should read and understand contracts generated by owners. In addition, the project manager must ask someone else in the firm to read the agreement. Depending on the design firm, this "second set of eyes" might be those of a firm's principal, someone in the firm's in-house legal department, or maybe the firm's attorney. In most firms, the project manager does not have the authority to sign an agreement anyway, so passing it on to someone who can is essential. In the previous chapter the project manager read the contract looking for paragraphs that defined the scope of work. For purposes of this chapter, the PM is looking for contract language that places the firm and/or the project at greater risk.

Avoid Contract Language That Increases Risk

Some contract provisions can be deal breakers, meaning that accepting them imparts such great risk to the project that it might just be better not to do the project at all. Two common deal-breaker clauses that owners like to insert in contracts are:

- Indemnity clauses that require the design firm to indemnify (assure, underwrite, hold harmless) and defend the owner against all claims, not just those caused by the design firm's negligence
- Guarantees, warranties, or certification clauses that require the design firm to guarantee, warrant, or certify things and work that are beyond the firm's control

Some words should be avoided because they inherently increase risk by expanding the responsibility of the design firm beyond that normally associated with professional practice. Words such as *certify, ensure, guarantee, insure, maximize, optimize,* and *supervise* can carry with them knockout punches. Before accepting the use of these words in the contract, obtain legal advice.

Avoid Unacceptable Risks

The project manager must identify potential risks to the project that are so significant that they cannot be accepted. For example, I have been told more than once by clients that they did not think a geotechnical report was necessary. What they really meant was they did not want to pay for one. On rare occasions, the client was correct: information regarding soil-bearing pressure and subsurface soil conditions was not important because the success of the project did not rest on having the information that a geotechnical report would provide. For many design projects, however, this information is crucial to the project's success. Not conducting a geotechnical investigation greatly increases the uncertainty about the soil conditions and the foundation design and, therefore, the risk to the project. There is an old joke among geotechnical engineers about the Leaning Tower of Pisa and what could have been, had there been geotechnical consultants back in 1173 when the design and construction of the tower began.

PMs must avoid unacceptable risks. If a client insists on omitting or doing something that dramatically increases the likelihood that something will go wrong, the PM needs to advise the client of the seriousness of the action. If the client continues to insist, then the PM should solicit help from others in the firm, a principal for example, who might prove more persuasive. On occasions I have asked for help from a firm principal in dissuading a client PM from pursuing some risky course of action. Many client PMs are much more willing to listen to and heed the advice from higher management, even if it is not from their own management, than they are to listen to the advice from another project manager.

By the way, the name of the architect responsible for the Leaning Tower of Pisa is not known. Some historians think it might have been Bonanno Pisano, an architect practicing in the area at the time. Others say it was Diotisalvi, the architect of the nearby Baptistery. Still others are persuaded that it was the architect Biduino because there are similarities between the Tower's ornamentation and other buildings known to be by Biduino. We will probably never know the architect's true name. But if a PM recklessly agrees to high-risk ventures and something goes terribly wrong, there is little doubt that his or her name will be remembered by the client and design firm for a long time.

Often the client is the most insistent on a dubious course of action. Ironically, the client is often the loudest complainer and quickest to point the finger at the design professional when the unsound action leads to disaster. For example, I am aware of a project where a client insisted that a 20-year-old soil report for one of its nearby facilities was good enough for its new adjacent facility. During building excavation, the contractor hit rock that could not be dug out using conventional earthmoving equipment. The client wound up writing a large unexpected change order to remove the rock.

Use Fee Types Appropriate for Services Provided

Some projects are better defined at the outset than others are. Some are so amorphous that it is not possible to know in advance exactly how long they will take to complete. Others are defined with considerable degrees of precision, including detailed objectives, programs, and schedule requirements. Project risk varies accordingly. Depending on project circumstances, certain project fee structures increase risk while others reduce it.

Many different types of fee structures are used in the contracting of design services. The five most common are described as follows.

Lump Sum (also called Fixed Price). With lump-sum contracts, a firm, fixed price is given to perform all the services required to complete the work. If the design firm spends less than the lump-sum amount, the firm receives the lump-sum amount and the money not spent drops directly to the project's bottom line as profit. Of course, if the firm spends more than the lump-sum amount, the project loses money.

Payment is linked to contract-defined deliverables—phases, reports, drawings, specifications, cost estimates, etc. Payment is often based on the percentage of the job that is complete. For example, if the contract states that a 50 percent submittal is required and it is made, including all the deliverables defined for that submittal, the design firm is entitled to invoice for 50 percent and receive payment for 50 percent of the lump sum, minus any contract-stipulated retainage if applicable. Retainage is the amount withheld by the owner—usually a percentage such as 10 percent—from periodic payments as security for the design firm's performance over the life of a project or until the design firm meets specific contract-defined milestones.

Lump-sum contracts are mainly used when the design project is well defined. If the project is not well defined, lump sums can be fraught with risk because poorly defined projects tend to take unexpected twists and turns that can increase the costs of design. Lump-sum contracts are relatively easy to administer for the design firm's and the client's project manager. Generally, invoices do not require backup that documents how labor hours were spent or material costs were incurred. Payment is based on clearly defined phases and deliverables.

Time and Materials (also called T&M). Time and materials is a fee structure by which the design firm is paid for time and materials spent, meaning it is paid for labor and its other direct costs (ODCs), such as printing, mailing, etc. Hourly labor rates are negotiated and established in advance of performing the work. In T&M contracts, labor rates can be fully loaded, meaning that they include all salary-related expenses (SREs), with overhead and profit built into the hourly rates, or they can be based on employee hourly salary rates multiplied by an agreed-on figure that includes SREs, overhead, and profit. Some T&M contracts allow design firms to mark up consultants (add a service or handling charge) by a negotiated percentage— 5 percent and 10 percent are common markup percentages. Generally, ODCs, such as printing costs and postage, cannot be marked up.

T&M contracts can be very good contracts for design firms because it is impossible to go over budget with a T&M contract. Every labor hour spent is paid for by the client. As long as the negotiated rates and/or multipliers are enough to cover a design firm's costs and profit, it is just about impossible to lose. Unlike with lump-sum contracts, it is not possible to improve a project's percentage of profit with a T&M contract. This is because the percent of profit is fixed, built right into the hourly rates or multiplier.

T&M contracts are generally used when it is difficult or impossible to determine a scope of work in advance. They are a bit more difficult to administer than lump-sum contracts because invoices require backup, showing labor hours spent and direct costs. If some direct costs or labor hours are challenged by the client, payment can be held up. Sometimes challenged costs are denied outright and payment for them is never received. Because the project's profit percentage is fixed, having several challenged and denied costs can take a significant bite out of a project's profitability. With a T&M job, there is no way to make it up, either.

Time and Materials with a Maximum-Not-to-Exceed. There is a very popular variation of the T&M fee structure called time and materials with a maximum-not-to-exceed. From an owner's point of view, straight T&M contracts are a lot like a blank check. Whatever the design firm does, the owner must pay for. From the owner's perspective, there seems to be little incentive for the design firm to be efficient at what it does, for it gets paid for every hour everyone works. Time and materials with a maximum-not-to-exceed solves this problem and, consequently, many owners prefer it. With this type of contract, the firm is paid for labor hours spent and for its ODCs, with or without markups as stipulated by the contract. But the contract has a maximum dollar amount that cannot be exceeded unless there is a change of scope and a subsequent contract amendment. Many owners prefer this contract type to the lump-sum contract because it eliminates the possibility of the design firm receiving a windfall profit should it actually take far less time to finish the project than was originally agreed to.

From the perspective of many design firm project managers, these are the most deflating types of contracts to manage financially because there is virtually no way to win. To maximize profit, the contract amount must be hit exactly without going over, which is nearly impossible. Going over the maximum-not-to-exceed amount cuts into profit. Running under adversely affects the project's gross income and profitability, because the monies associated with the hours that are not spent are not realized. Hitting the maximum-not-to-exceed amount yields only the contract-stipulated profit, which is generally somewhere between 8 percent to 15 percent. Additional profit, as a reward for running an effective and efficient project, is not possible with T&M with a maximum-not-to-exceed contract. Such contracts tend to run counter to the entrepreneurial spirit of many good project managers. On the flip side, design professionals are not hired for their entrepreneurial spirit. They are hired to provide competent professional design services, so some might argue, why reward them for being an effective capitalist?

Cost Plus Fixed Fee. With a cost plus fixed fee contract, the design firm is paid for all its costs, labor, and materials. However, the labor costs do not carry profit. Profit is a negotiated fixed amount that does not vary with actual costs. With this type of contract, the amount of labor and ODCs required to accomplish the specified work are estimated. The actual cost may vary but the fee—profit—is fixed. If for some reason it takes more hours and/or costs to accomplish the work, the firm will be paid for the labor and costs but the amount of profit will not be adjusted. The profit, as the name implies, is fixed.

This type of fee has advantages for both the owner and the design firm. The design firm—meaning the project manager—has every incentive to run the project effectively and efficiently because the percent of profit increases if fewer hours are spent. This benefits the owner as well, for the owner winds up spending less money overall. The situation is win-win. Should the project go over budget, the design firm loses profit as a percentage of the total costs. While the owner is out additional monies, the owner is not paying any more profit to the design firm. Neither the owner nor the design firm benefit from the project going over budget, although some might argue that the owner benefits less than the design firm, because the design firm's costs are still covered by the owner.

Cost Plus Fixed Fee with a Guaranteed Maximum Price (GMP). This contract type is a version of the cost plus fixed fee contract described previously except that the contract does have a guaranteed maximum amount. If the design firm goes over the maximum amount, it is not compensated for its costs. This contract type has all the advantages of the cost plus fixed fee contract, but it protects the owner from severe cost overruns, should there be any.

Provide More Comprehensive Services

Risk can be reduced by providing more comprehensive services. Fuller services often can provide better and more comprehensive quality and can better address the entire breadth of the project. Of particular help is providing construction support services in addition to design services. By providing both, it is easier to check and catch mistakes that may have been made during design.

Sometimes nagging little mistakes are missed during the final quality-control check of the design process. Often these are more likely to be caught by the design firm than by a third-party construction management (CM) firm because the design firm has a better understanding of the intent of the documents as well as their literal meaning. Reviewing submittals and answering contractors' requests for information (RFIs) allow the design firm one final opportunity to check and review materials and systems before they are incorporated into the construction work or, literally, cast in concrete.

Identify Excluded As Well As Included Services

Contracts for design services include a scope of services, a detailed description of those services that are required to be performed by the design firm. Contracts can be written to exclude work as well. Often this is helpful because it reduces the risk of misunderstanding between the owner and the design professional. In some cases, the owner may assume certain services are included because they were included the last time or because the owner believes they are common design services, when, in fact, they are not. For example, many projects include programming services, but not all do. Most design firms consider programming services as additional services. While they are glad to provide them, they do not necessarily provide them as a matter of course. The AIA, by the way, also considers programming services as additional services.

Some projects require surveys; others do not. In some cases, the owner provides the survey; in others, the design professional does. Some projects do not require a survey at all. The same can be said for geotechnical investigations, traffic studies, hazardous-materials investigations, and acoustical studies. Services such as these can be provided by the owner, the design professional, or not at all. When there is doubt, it should be made clear in the contract what services the design firm is providing and what services it is not.

If the owner is to provide certain documents, such as a geotechnical report, survey, etc., this should be spelled out in the contract. If the design firm has offered certain services that it thinks are required, but the owner has declined, it is a good idea to list these in the contract as well.

I recall a project for a bus company that included an extensive bus wash facility. Even though the bus wash system included a wash-water recycle feature, our design team was concerned about the amount of dirty wash water that would be discharged into the city's sanitary sewer system, a system that we suspected might be near capacity based on the experience of some design team members. This suggested that our project might require large and costly holding tanks to store the dirty wash water before discharging it at a metered flow rate that was acceptable to the city. Because we were not sure at the time whether such holding tanks were required or not, we did not include the design of them in our fee proposal. Rather, we specifically excluded them with an explanation of why, saying we would be happy to design them if and when we determined that they were required. Design of the holding tanks was specifically excluded in the contract.

Specify How Disputes Will Be Resolved

Lawsuits can be very stressful. In addition, they expose the project and the design firm to enormous financial uncertainty that, as this chapter has explained, dramatically increases the project risk. As the Design Professionals Insurance Corporation (DPIC) explains in its book *DPIC's Contract Guide:*

> When a claim is filed, it signals the beginning of an exceedingly rough journey that will, in all probability, last several years. The impact can be devastating. The costs in lost staff time, the uninsured expenses associated with defending oneself . . . can be ruinous to a professional practice.[38]

Lawsuits can be stressful to clients as well, for the very same reasons described previously. It is an old adage but true, "No one wins in a lawsuit." Consequently, design professionals, owners, and contractors have explored various alternative dispute resolution techniques. It is well worth considering a contract clause requiring one or more of these dispute resolution techniques in lieu of the alternative: a long, drawn-out court case. Three resolution techniques that are commonly used in design contracts are:

- Partnering
- Mediation
- Arbitration

Partnering is a series of facilitator-lead team-building sessions that include the owner, contractor, and design professional. The first session takes place before the project begins and subsequent sessions take place at regular intervals throughout the project. Partnering's intent is to define goals that are common to all parties, improve communication among the parties, and eliminate the "us-against-them" project mentality before it forms. Partnering sessions promote fair play, mutual respect, and understanding among the project participants with the goal of heading off serious disputes that can lead to hostility and eventually to lawsuits.

I have participated in a number of partnering sessions. In my experience, they are only successful when all the key team members truly embrace the process and actively try to make it work. If partnering is treated as "just one of the useless things that has to be done," then it does not work. At a minimum, good partnering sessions must accomplish the following:

- All key team members commit to cooperation and agree to communication openly and honestly.
- Establish the overall collaborative project objectives (often summarized in a mission statement).
- Establish lines of communication, including an issues resolution procedure.
- Foster a win-win problem-solving attitude.

- Develop methods for measuring whether the overall objectives are being met.
- Agree to consider creative ways to control costs.
- Establish a follow-up process—set regular or milestone meetings to access progress and fine-tune procedures.

Mediation is a voluntary method of resolving disputes by which the parties agree to a resolution themselves. To help them agree, a third-party mediator, agreed to by all parties, is assigned and acts as the go-between, helping the parties negotiate an acceptable resolution. Mediation is usually not binding on the parties involved, meaning that the parties do not have to accept a resolution and the resolution is not court-enforceable. Filing a lawsuit is available to all parties as a final resort. However, if the parties buy in to the mediation process and agree to it by contract, most parties are likely to accept the outcome. The AIA's Standard Form of Agreement Between Owner and Architect (B141) recommends mediation as the first step in dispute resolution. Should mediation fail, B141 next recommends arbitration.

Arbitration is the most formal of the three methods described here. In arbitration the opposing parties, generally with their attorneys, present their cases before one or more individuals who are empowered to render a decision. Most arbitrators are architects, engineers, and constructors themselves, so they are very familiar with the often complex technical issues that bear on a design and/or a construction-related dispute. Most arbitrators are members of the American Arbitration Association (AAA), which is an organization with a long and reputable history of resolving disputes.

Many, but not all, contract clauses that call for arbitration call for binding arbitration, meaning that the decision rendered by the arbitrator(s) is a court-enforceable decision. Arbitration does not, however, follow the same rules of evidence as do civil courts. For example, arbitrators can and do permit hearsay testimony and the admission of irrelevant testimony and evidence. They can refuse evidence and render judgments not based on legal principles. They do not even have to abide by the terms of the contract and they generally are not required to state the reasons behind their decisions.

Inform the Client of Potential Risks

As stated in the first sentence of this chapter, design projects are inherently risky. Some risks cannot be avoided. A project manager must educate an owner regarding risks that cannot be avoided. This way, should problems occur, the client will not be surprised and/or disappointed with the PM or the design firm.

I recall a small residential project from many years ago. It was a kitchen and dining room remodel and addition. The husband-and-wife client had recently bought a 30-year-old house and decided to redo the kitchen and expand the dining room. They had never undertaken a remodeling project before. They had never hired an architect or a contractor. Drawings were prepared, a contractor was hired, a building permit received, and construction began. During demolition, the contractor uncovered illegal wiring behind the base cabinets in the kitchen. Evidently, a previous owner had tried a little handy work of his own. The wiring, which served some of the above countertop outlets, had to be replaced. The contractor gave the owner a price for an electrician to remove the illegal wiring and install new wiring. The owner expected the contractor to do the work for free. The contractor explained that it was extra work because he had no way of knowing the illegal wiring was there. Next, the owner asked the architect, me, if he shouldn't pay for the new wiring, since he "missed it" on his drawings. It was not until then that I explained the risks involved in remodeling and eventually convinced the clients that they should pay to have the illegal wiring removed and new wiring installed. I learned a lesson: explain to clients, in advance, the risks inherent in remodeling projects.

Remodeling projects have many uncertainties. Hiding within walls, above ceilings, and buried within crawl spaces are frequently unforeseen and unforeseeable conditions that can affect the cost of construction. While it might be possible to take a building apart during the design phase to uncover the surprises, from a practical point of view this is rarely done. In addition, the cost of doing so may actually exceed the cost of dealing with the unknown conditions if and when they are uncovered during construction. It is wise for the project manager to explain the inherent risks associated with remodeling projects to owners who are unfamiliar with the uncertainties of such project types and prepare them for the likelihood of change orders during construction.

Choose Consultants Carefully

It is a wedding. Do not make it a shotgun wedding. Marry out of love.

Many design firms select consultants because the consultant is an "owner favorite" or the consultant meets a Disadvantaged Business Enterprise (DBE) participation goal or small-business set-aside requirement that the client wishes to achieve. Choosing consultants for these reasons alone—a shotgun wedding—can significantly increase project risk.

Choosing new consultants to work with is much like hiring a new employee. The PM should choose consultants who are qualified and who strengthen the design team. The consultant's performance will affect the project and will reflect on the project manager. Make it a good reflection.

Before selecting new consultants, the PM should interview them; discuss their qualifications and past work experience; visit their offices and, if possible, meet their staff members who are likely to be assigned a key role in the PM's project. The PM should ask for and speak with the consultant's references, and determine that the consultant has the necessary professional licenses and can meet the project's insurance requirements. Finally, and perhaps most important, the PM must decide if the consultant will be a good fit with the rest of the design team.

Do Not Start Production of Contract Documents Until the Design Is Well Defined and Approved by the Client

As discussed in Chapter 5, the design process is iterative and the production of contract documents (CDs) is linear. These are two entirely different work approaches. The transition from one to the other is a critical moment in the life of a project. If the handoff is not clean and crisp, risk to the project can increase.

The iterative design process must identify and define all the major characteristics and components of the project. It forms the foundation on which the contract documents are built. If the design is poorly defined or major portions are left out or the client makes changes, these design issues will have to be addressed and resolved during the production of the CDs. The production of CDs, however, uses a step-by-step work approach that is not conducive to iterative problem solving. If CD production continues while major design issues are being developed or revisited, some production work may have to be redone. Should production stop, it can be costly to both the project and the design firm. It can adversely affect the quality of the project. Stopping a major project in the middle of CDs can leave many staff members without work. Prolonged stops can be very painful to a design firm's finances.

Consequently, the project manager should not start production of CDs until the design phase is complete. This means that all the major design objectives have been addressed and resolved, at least conceptually. It also means that the client understands the design and has approved it for production.

It is best to get the client's approval in writing. Some contracts require the owner to approve the design phase work and issue a notice to proceed before the production of contract documents begins. Contracts with this provision help protect both the design firm and the client from untimely and costly changes to the work during the contract document phase. If there is no such clause, the PM can request that the client write a letter or memo (even an e-mail) stating that the client agrees to the design solution and authorizes the production of contract documents to begin.

Avoid Running Projects without Budget and Schedule Contingencies

Trying to run a project without contingencies is like trying to walk a tightrope without a net. Why take the risk? No project manager is good enough to know exactly what is going to happen during the life of a project. While many risks can be managed, they cannot be eliminated completely. Without budget and schedule contingencies, there is no way for the project to absorb the shock if the unexpected happens.

As a rule of thumb, it is a good idea to set aside at least 10 percent of a project's budget as a contingency. As the project proceeds, this contingency can be moved to plug holes where needed. The 10 percent rule of thumb is not an absolute. Every project manager has to use judgment based on the specific project. Some projects may have greater uncertainties and require more contingency. Small projects with just one discipline may be fine with a 5 percent contingency. But experience has taught me that 10 percent is a good, general minimum contingency with which to start most projects.

Developing a scheduling contingency is much more difficult. There are many unknowns in most project schedules. Not only does the PM have to control the design team's work schedule, the PM has to allocate schedule time for client input and reviews as well. In general, it is a good approach to add days to each phase of the work. The number of days depends on the complexity, size, and duration of the project, but adding 10 percent more days to each phase is good start. The PM should get the client's opinion of how long it will take for reviews. Clients are frequently late with their review comments. If the client says two weeks, the PM might consider adding an additional half week or full week to the schedule. By taking this approach, a comfortable contingency is built in throughout the length of the project schedule.

CHAPTER 6 CHECKLIST

Risk is the measure of the potential threats and uncertainties that can affect a project. Risk increases in direct proportion to the number of threats and uncertainties—the greater their number, the greater the risk. The project manager must manage risk by minimizing project threats and uncertainties. This chapter offers suggestions for managing various risks, which are summarized in the checklist that follows:

❑ Have I and/or the design firm worked with this client before and was the relationship successful?

❑ Have I worked successfully with this design team before?

❑ Is this project of a type and size with which we have experience and were we successful with this type of project before?

❑ Is the project contract based on a nationally recognized standardized contract or is it our firm's standard contract?

❑ Do I understand the provisions of the contract?

❑ Are there clauses in the contract that increase risk, such as indemnity and warranty clauses that require the design firm to indemnify the owner against all claims or warrant work that is beyond the firm's capability to control?

❑ Are there words in the contract that increase risk, such as *certify, ensure, guarantee, insure, maximize, optimize?*

❑ Is the type of fee appropriate for the kind of project?

❑ Is the contract clear or ambiguous regarding what services are included or excluded?

❑ Does the contract specify how disputes are to be resolved?

Here are additional questions the project manager should ask to reduce project risk:

❑ Have I chosen my consultants carefully? Have I successfully worked with them before?

❑ Before I start work on the contract documents is the design well defined and approved by the client?

❑ Do I have an adequate project budget and schedule contingency?

THE NEXT CHAPTER

This chapter did not address two additional potential project risks that the project manager must manage. They are the project's construction cost and the project's design budget. Properly managing these two budgets is essential to successfully managing a project. The next two chapters will look at project construction cost and design budget control and suggest various ways of managing them.

7

CONSTRUCTION
COST CONTROL

Design projects generally have two cost budgets that the project manager must control. One is the budget for doing the design work itself. The other is the budget for constructing the project as defined by the design and construction documents. This chapter discusses the importance of construction cost control and suggests ways of controlling it during the design process.

Many sophisticated clients who build facilities on a more-or-less regular basis frequently develop their initial project budgets before the design professional is selected and before any design work is ever done. Client project budgets generally contain several component parts. They have a:

- Project construction budget—the maximum amount the client wants (hopes) to spend to have the project built
- Project design budget—the maximum amount the client wants (hopes) to spend for the design and preparation of the construction documents for the project

- Project administration budget—the amount the client has allotted for its own internal costs to manage the project
- Construction support services budget—the amount the client has budgeted for construction inspection, testing, review of submittals, etc.
- Project contingency budget—the amount the client has set aside for design and/or construction changes
- Total project budget—the sum of the budgets described previously

Sometimes a client's project construction budget is based on direct experience from building similar projects in the past. The client updates its actual cost data for inflation, develops a square-foot cost, and uses this to determine the budgetary construction cost for its similar upcoming project. Other times a client's construction budget is based on a space program study and estimate prepared by another consultant, a space programmer for example. Sometimes the construction budget is based on historical data regarding square-foot costs for similar projects culled from various sources.

Historical cost data frequently is available from cost data handbooks, such as R. S. Means cost data reference manuals (Means). Means publishes a series of cost data reference books that include cost data based on the historical costs of construction for various project types and sizes. Means and other reference manuals include data about professional design fees expressed as percentages of construction cost for various general building-type categories. The magazine *Engineering News Record* (ENR) also contains useful construction cost data including an ENR Index that allows construction cost comparisons using construction data from different years.

Sometimes project budgets are determined by public referenda—how much the public is willing to spend for a particular project. In such cases, there is frequently a disconnect between project scope and budget. The actual needs of the project are often far greater than the referendum budget can support.

An example of this is the San Francisco Bay Area's rapid transit system called BART (short for Bay Area Rapid Transit district). By 1962, the California state legislature and Bay Area voters approved bond measures totaling $792 million for the construction of BART. They also agreed to an additional funding source of $115 million from bridge tolls from the San Francisco/Oakland Bay Bridge. As early as mid-1961, however, the project design consultants were already estimating that the project would cost upwards of $1.3 billion, a $400 million disconnect.

Some projects start with the client having a well-defined project and a specific dollar amount budgeted for the construction cost. In such cases, the cost to construct the project is sometimes refined during the early phases of project programming and conceptual design, through the combined work of the design firm's project team and client. Such refinements frequently result in construction budgets that are higher than originally estimated.

In other cases, the client does not have a well-defined project at the outset, only a general idea of what it wants. In these situations, the design team, again working with the client, develops the project's program, concept, and associated construction budget that reflects the desired scope of work.

Regardless of the scenario, at some point a construction budget is determined. Once it is, the project manager must manage the design process from that point forward so that the project can be built within the construction budget.

THE CONSTRUCTION BUDGET

There is one number all clients remember. It is the first construction cost they hear from their design professional. Clients may forget program requirements or decisions that have been made. But they do not seem to forget the first construction cost estimate. So it had better be a good number. If it is not, it very well may come back to haunt the project manager and the design firm.

As a general rule, it is a good idea not to tell the client the construction cost for a project when there is insufficient information or too many variables that can affect the cost of construction. The information needed to give an informed answer varies from project to project, but generally it includes such factors as the project's intended use, scope, functional space program, size, quality, geographic location, site conditions, construction bidding climate, and schedule. While the design professional may be a better estimator than the client, any number given with insufficient information and too many variables is not much more than a guess. There is no point in jeopardizing the project from the outset by irresponsible guessing. It is much better to put some thought into the first number the client will hear because that is the number the client will remember.

A few years ago, I was the PM for a design team that won a project to design an administration building for a city in California. Our design team's first task was to validate a space program and construction cost estimate for the project that had been prepared by another consultant a few years earlier. Dividing the estimated construction cost by the total square footage contained in the space program yielded the estimated cost per square foot for the project. Using a cost-per-square-foot rule of thumb, along with my experience with this type of facility, I quickly realized that the estimated construction cost was too low, approximately 50 percent too low. I knew immediately that I had to tell the client my concern. I backed up my assessment with a spreadsheet listing similar projects, their sizes, bid prices, bid dates, building types, and functions. Before I told the client, I fully expected that the client's project manager would be very disappointed, maybe even become a bit upset. His reaction surprised me, however. He did not get upset or even sound disappointed. He told me that he suspected as much and now, with our firm's assessment and the spreadsheet showing comparable construction costs, he had enough "ammunition" to get the project's budget increased.

The reason I knew not to hesitate about telling the client the bad news is because I learned a lesson about project construction budgets many years earlier from another PM's mistake.

Before doing any construction cost estimating, the PM told the client that its custom film-processing lab would cost x amount of dollars. The PM picked the number because he knew it was in line with what the client wanted to hear. The design was completed, the project was bid (there were only two bidders), and the lower bid was approximately two times higher than the estimate. The client was not pleased. Trying to soothe ruffled feathers, the PM reminded the client that during the course of the design the client had added scope to the project. While true, the PM did not warn the client of the effect these changes would have on the cost of construction as the changes occurred. In the client's opinion, a film-processing lab that cost twice what the client could afford was useless. The client stopped paying the design firm and the project ended in the hands of lawyers.

This story illustrates a few important points about controlling a project's construction cost. First, as already discussed, the initial construction cost estimate must be based on sound information, specific to the particular project. Second, sometimes the number may not be what the client wants to hear. Nevertheless, it is what the client *needs* to hear. Third, changes in scope can affect the construction cost. Sometimes their impact is small and consequently overlooked. But if enough small changes are strung together, they can become significant. The client must be made aware of the construction cost implications of changes. Fourth, the bidding climate affects the construction cost. In the previous example, there were only two bidders, which very likely affected the bids. Saylor Consulting Group, a construction cost estimating firm, publishes a construction cost estimating manual yearly. Although the following does not appear in the most recent edition, Saylor's *2000 Current Construction Costs* book states:

> Examination of a large number of bids received would indicate that the deviation from engineering estimates produced from complete drawings, using the pricing in this resource, is as follows:

1 bid	+15% to +40%
2–3 bids	+8% to +12%
4–5 bids	–4% to +4%
6–7 bids	–7% to –5%
8 or more bids	–12% to 8%[39]

A recent and dramatic example of a failure to control construction costs is the Scottish Parliament Building in Edinburgh, Scotland (see Figure 7.1), designed by the late, world-renowned architect Enric Miralles. In June of 1998, it was originally programmed at 170,000 square feet with an estimated construction cost of $75 million. The final building, completed six years later in 2004, has an area of 325,000 square feet (almost double the original) and a staggering price tag of $830 million (over ten times the original estimate!). The building has led the architectural critic Charles Jencks to comment:

> The result is one of the most interesting, vilified, costly and marvelous buildings of our time.[40]

The masterful artistic success of the Scottish Parliament Building is tainted by its tremendous cost overruns, as reflected in the very title of *Architectural Record*'s February 2005 cover story, "Scottish Parliament: Enric Miralles's Bittersweet Achievement."[41]

FIGURE 7.1 Scottish Parliament

The architectural and artistic success of the Scottish Parliament Building is tarnished by its extraordinary cost overruns. Enric Miralles, architect. Photograph by the author.

Designing to cost is a primary objective for most projects and, as discussed in Chapter 2, a fundamental goal of project management. To do so, the best approach is to:

- Develop a realistic construction cost budget from the outset.
- Break down the construction cost budget into a budgetary cost model.
- Lead, manage, and monitor the development of the project so that the design reflects the cost model.

BUDGETARY COST MODEL

A budgetary cost model is a breakdown of the overall estimated construction cost into major building components, materials, and systems. It establishes cost targets for each major building component, providing a cost framework within which to develop the design. It is the baseline against which the design and selection of building materials and systems can be evaluated for their cost appropriateness. If a particular building system or material is within the parameters of its budgetary cost, it is a suitable, cost-effective choice. If not, then other systems or materials should be considered and evaluated for their cost appropriateness. Figure 7.2 illustrates a typical budgetary cost model.

FIGURE 7.2 Typical Budgetary Cost Model

Budgetary Cost Model

CSI Division	MATERIAL AND SYSTEMS	BUDGETS
3	CONCRETE (FOUNDATION & SLAB-ON-GRADE)	$100,000
4	MASONRY (CONCRETE BLOCK WALLS)	$80,000
5	STEEL FRAMING & ARCHITECTURAL METALS	$60,000
6	ROUGH, FINISH CARPENTRY & ARCHITECTURAL WOODWORK	$25,000
7	THERMAL & MOISTURE PROTECTION (ROOFING & INSULATION)	$50,000
8	DOORS AND WINDOWS	$50,000
9	FINISHES	$125,000
10	SPECIALTIES	$20,000
21	FIRE SPRINKLER AND FIRE ALARM SYSTEM	$50,000
22	PLUMBING	$50,000
23	MECHANICAL (HEATING, VENTILATING, AND AIR CONDITIONING)	$75,000
26	ELECTRICAL (POWER, LIGHTING, COMMUNICATIONS)	$100,000
30	SITE WORK & INFRASTRUCTURE	$200,000
	SUBTOTAL OF MATERIAL & SYSTEMS BUDGETS	$985,000
	GENERAL CONDITIONS AT 8%	$78,800
	CONTRACTORS OVERHEAD AND PROFIT AT 12%	$128,000
	SUBTOTAL	$1,192,000
	COST MODEL ESTIMATING CONTINGENCY AT 20%	$238,000
	SUBTOTAL	$1,430,000
	ESCALATION TO THE MIDPOINT OF CONSTRUCTION AT 5%	$72,000
	TOTAL (rounded to nearest ten thousand)	$1,500,000

Note that the budgetary cost model in Figure 7.2 includes an estimating contingency. In this case, the contingency is 20 percent. Depending on the project, this percentage may vary. If the project is complicated or a number of unknowns exist, a larger contingency may be required. If the cost model is set up without a contingency, when one component goes over budget, another must be adjusted downward so that the overall project stays on budget—like that old saying, "Robbing Peter to pay Paul." Because this is often difficult to do, it is far safer to include a contingency.

In addition, the cost model includes typical construction contractor costs. Budgetary cost models that include construction-related costs are better models than those that ignore these costs because they more realistically reflect the actual costs of construction. Note, also, that the cost model includes an escalation line item. Often a considerable time delay occurs between when a project is conceived and when it is built. Construction projects are not immune from inflation.

A realistic construction cost budget and budgetary cost model should be determined as close to a project's outset as possible. It should be based on an understanding of the project's requirements, its use, size, quality, geographic location, site conditions, construction bidding climate, and schedule.

Generally, the PM should consult with members of the design team to establish this budget. It may also be necessary to hire a construction cost estimating consultant to assist in developing a realistic construction cost estimate and budgetary cost model.

CHAPTER 7 CHECKLIST

To control a project's construction cost, it is worth asking:

❏ Did the design team and I put considerable thought into the first construction cost estimate we told the client because it is the one the client will remember most?

❏ Is the estimated construction cost realistic?
❏ Did I develop a budgetary cost model for the project and did I share it with the design team?
❏ Is the design team designing the project within the cost parameters of the cost model?

8

DESIGN BUDGET CONTROL

In addition to controlling the project construction cost, the project manager is expected to perform the design work within the design fee or design budget. If the project design fee is lump sum or T&M with a maximum-not-to-exceed (see Chapter 6 for definitions of these two fee types), the client has transferred most, if not all, of the risk of performing the design work within budget to the design firm. As long as the scope of work does not change, the client is insulated from design cost overruns and the design firm must eat the overruns. Design firms generally have little appetite for this. The project manager must prevent this force-feeding.

Whether design professionals like it or not, many clients use percentage rules of thumb when evaluating and determining the reasonableness of a design firm's proposed fee. Design fees have a market value.

The process of establishing a budget for design and production work is as much art as science. A project's final design budget is generally a nuanced compromise based on a combination of many factors, including an understanding of the scope of work, experience with similar past projects, input from the team members who will be doing the work, past experience with the client, and what the market will bear. As stated previously, design work has a market value.

Project managers frequently participate with the design firm's upper management or business development staff in winning projects and in establishing or negotiating design fees. On other occasions, the project manager may be handed a budget for a particular project based on a design fee that has been determined (negotiated) by others in the firm. A design budget established this way is sometimes called a *top-down budget* because it was developed by upper management or a business development staff and then passed down to the project manager and design team who will do the work. This happens more often than one might expect, so often that PMs use the term *over the transom* for projects they receive where the scope of work and design budget have been established by someone else within the firm before the PM and design team ever see the project.

Another way of determining a project's budget is to build it from the bottom up. Bottom-up budgets begin with budget numbers prepared by the disciplines who will be performing the work. The disciplines generally express the work effort in hours, but dollars can be used. The PM combines the numbers received from the disciplines and then adds project management time, direct costs, consultant costs, any contingency that he or she feels may be necessary, and profit. Consultant costs are calculated by asking for fee proposals from the consultants. A bit of massaging and negotiating may be necessary, but a fee proposal prepared and negotiated in this manner is generally based on a more realistic understanding of the effort necessary to do the work than the top-down method of calculating provides.

Regardless of how the project manager receives the project, the PM is responsible for the financial success of the project. Over-the-transom projects must be designed within the pre-established top-down budget. Because the scope of work and budget are fixed before the PM receives the project, the PM has no choice but to plan the design work to fit the project's predetermined budget constraints.

When the PM has an opportunity to participate in project negotiations, it is possible to establish a budget that fits a mutually acceptable scope of work. During negotiations, neither the budget nor the scope of work are rigidly fixed. One or the other or both can usually be adjusted to some degree. If successfully negotiated, a project budget can be established that is a realistic reflection of the work to be performed. Some commons items that can be negotiated are:

- Reducing the number of design alternatives to be studied
- Reducing the number of submittals. Instead of 30 percent, 50 percent, 75 percent, 90 percent, and 100 percent submittals, consider negotiating a 35 percent submittal, 80 percent and 100 percent. This reduces the number of submittals and therefore the design costs associated with making so many submittals. The 35 percent submittal (roughly equal to preliminary design) will establish the general layout, appearance, site, and building systems. The 80 percent submittal gives the client an opportunity to confirm that the construction documents reflect the design intent and to make comments before the contract documents are finalized.
- Reducing the number of meetings. Some clients love meetings and hold too many of them. A lot of time and money is spent by design firms preparing for, attending, and then documenting the results of the meetings.
- Reducing the scope of work. A direct relationship exists between the size of the scope of work and the amount of money spent preparing the design. For example, perhaps the scope can be reduced by deleting the perspective rendering and the design of the landscape partitions. Instead of three different schematic design alternatives,

maybe two would be acceptable. See if the client has the freedom to hire the geotechnical engineer and/or the surveyor directly.

SETTING UP THE PROJECT FINANCIALS

Once the design budget is set, the fee must be broken down into work tasks and their budgets. If the design fee was built from the bottom up, the project manager has most of the budget information already, for it was developed by the PM and the disciplines in the first place. It may need some adjusting, however, depending on how the fee negotiations went. If the budget was prepared top-down, the project manager will have to divide the fee by discipline and obtain buy-in from the various discipline leads. This can be a challenge with top-down budgets, particularly if the fee is "tight," that is, barely enough to do the work.

Once the discipline and task budgets have been determined, the breakdowns must be entered into the firm's project cost accounting system. Most design firms have well-established computerized project accounting procedures and policies that they expect all their project managers to follow. Most firms assign job numbers to projects. Often these job numbers have managerial information embedded within the number. For example, some of the digits may represent the year, others the client type, project type, or branch office doing the work, etc. Usually a firm's accounting software allows each project job number to associate additional hierarchical subordinate numbers or codes with it. These codes become the task codes that form the work breakdown structure (WBS) for the project. A well-planned project WBS provides the work plan, accounting, feedback, and monitoring information that a project manager needs to run and manage the project.

For the information to be as useful as possible, the WBS must first be set up properly. The following guidelines will help in setting up meaningful and useful work breakdown structures:

- The WBS should relate to the contract requirements and use similar terminology.
- The WBS should be hierarchical—budgets should roll up so that they cannot be counted twice.
- The WBS should be no more complicated than is absolutely necessary to manage the project.
- Staff must intuitively understand the codes to which they are to charge their time.

SAMPLE PROJECT

An example will help illustrate some essential points about a project's design fee and how to set up a project work breakdown structure. The XYZ project, a hypothetical multidisciplinary design project, has the following contract-defined criteria:

- Project has a lump-sum contract.
- Project has three contract-defined design phases: 30 percent, 75 percent, and 100 percent.
- Before moving from one phase to the next, the client must give the design firm a written notice to proceed (NTP).

In addition to the contract criteria, the example assumes that all the design work will be done in-house. Two consultants are needed: a surveyor to prepare a site survey and a geotechnical engineer to prepare a soils report.

The budget for the XYZ project was built bottom-up, that is, the PM, disciplines, and consultants participated in developing the budget. Figure 8.1 shows a breakdown of the XYZ project design fee.

FIGURE 8.1   Breakdown of Design Fee

XYZ PROJECT—Breakdown of Design Fee	30%	75%	100%	Totals (hrs)	
Project Management	120	150	130	400	
Architectural	350	350	300	1,000	
Civil	100	150	150	400	
Structural	180	440	380	1,000	
Mechanical	110	260	130	500	
Electrical	80	190	230	500	Dollars
Totals	940	1,540	1,320	3,800	$380,000 *
				Contingency	$38,000
* Based on an average in-house rate of $100 per hour				Consultants	$60,000
				Direct Costs	$22,000
				Profit	$50,000
				Total Design Fee	$550,000

Breakdown of the design fee of a hypothetical multidisciplinary project into constituent budgets.

Figure 8.1 assumes an average hourly project charge rate of $100–for every hour an employee works on the project, $100 is charged to the project. In this case, the hourly rate covers the employee's salary, SREs, and the firm's overhead costs. It does not include profit. Profit is shown as a separate line item, located near the bottom of Figure 8.1.

Some firms include profit in their hourly rates while others do not. The PM needs to know how the design firm accounts for profit and must build the project budget in a manner consistent with the firm's accounting practices.

This project has a contingency equal to 10 percent of in-house labor. No PM is clever enough and no design team good enough to complete a half-million-dollar design project without a safety net. For a project of this size, a contingency of at least 10 percent is a reasonable amount to set aside. If a discipline needs more hours for some reason, the PM can dip into the contingency. Without a contingency, the only place the hours can come from is from another discipline–robbing one to pay another.

FIGURE 8.2 In-house Discipline Budgets

XYZ Project Discipline Budgets as Percentage of Fee	
Project Management	10.5 %
Architectural	26.3
Civil	10.5
Structural	26.3
Mechanical	13.2
Electrical	13.2
Total	100 %

Note:
Discipline percentages will vary depending on the type of project and project particulars. Generally, project management runs in the range of 8 percent to 15 percent of the total fee.

The in-house discipline budgets for the XYZ project shown as percentages.

On the top row of Figure 8.1, note the total budget of 400 hours for project management. Figure 8.2 shows the project management budget and the other in-house discipline budgets expressed as percentages. The budget for the project manager is 10.5 percent of the in-house design hours, which is about average. Although it varies from project to project, project management budgets for design projects generally run somewhere between 8 percent to 15 percent.

Rule-of-thumb percentages for the other disciplines are harder to come by, because so many variables are involved and every project is a bit different. This is why it is a good idea to build the design budget from the bottom up, with input from the various disciplines.

Figure 8.3 shows the design fee broken down by percent per phase. Note that only 25 percent of the fee is budgeted for the 30 percent design. Sixty-five percent is budgeted to reach the 75 percent level. This leaves 35 percent of the fee to finish the last 25 percent.

Generally, it is difficult and, therefore, expensive to finish up the last 10 percent of a design project. Prudent project

FIGURE 8.3   In-house Discipline Budgets

XYZ Project
Fee Breakdown per Phase

	30%	75%	100%	Totals
Totals by Phase (hours)	940	1,540	1,320	3,800
Totals by Phase (percent)	25	40	35	100%

The in-house discipline budgets for the XYZ project shown as percentages per project phase.

managers plan their projects knowing that it will take about 20 percent of the budget to finish the last 10 percent of the project.

Figure 8.4 takes the information presented in Figure 8.1 and adds to it the WBS charge codes.

Based on the WBS setup in Figure 8.4, a typical time-card charge code might be: 123456-75-S, meaning that the work was charged to job number 123456 by the structural group working on the 75 percent design. Note that the WBS codes recognize that the XYZ project contract has three phases and that the project is multidisciplinary. The budgets for all phases and disciplines are identified.

The information is not duplicated. Disciplines charge by discipline and by phase only. Also, the WBS structure is not unnecessarily complicated. It allows for simple tracking of the work by phase and by discipline, giving the PM the information needed to manage this relatively straightforward multidisciplinary project. Also, it is intuitively clear to each team member where to charge his or her time. This is important for a PM should not have to police every project every time-card day to make sure everyone is charging their work to the correct codes.

FIGURE 8.4 The XYZ Project Work Breakdown Structure

XYZ Project No.	Phase Codes	WBS Codes	WBS Budgets Hours	Dollars
123456	**30** (30% Design)	PM	120	
		A	350	
		C	100	
		S	180	
		M	110	
		E	80	
		CTS		$40,000
		ODC		7,000
		CON		9,400
			940	$56,400
	75 (75% Design)	PM	150	
		A	350	
		C	150	
		S	440	
		M	260	
		E	190	
		CTS		10,000
		ODC		9,000
		CON		15,400
			1,540	$34,400
	100 (100% Design)	PM	130	
		A	300	
		C	150	
		S	380	
		M	130	
		E	230	
		CTS		10,000
		ODC		6,000
		CON		13,200
			1,320	$29,200
		TOTALS	**3,800**	**$120,000**

WBS
A= Architecture
C= Civil
S= Structural
M= Mechanical
E= Electrical
CTS= Consultants
ODC= Other Direct Costs
CON= Contingency

Implied in the contract for the XYZ project is the possibility that the client can stop the work after each phase by not issuing the NTP for the next phase. Consequently, the project manager cannot let the design team get too far ahead. For example, at the end of 30 percent design, the design firm can invoice for 30 percent of the fee, but certainly not for 50 percent of it, even if 50 percent of the fee has been spent getting to 30 percent complete. To protect against this possibility, the PM needs to monitor how much money is being spent by phase. Because the work breakdown structure rolls up the discipline work by phases, it is relatively easy for the PM to keep track, provided he or she reviews the project financial reports on a regular basis.

EARNED VALUE

The earned value is the amount of the budget allotted to a particular task that has been accomplished and is, therefore, earned, regardless of the actual amount spent. For example, the XYZ project shows that the civil engineering discipline has a budget of 100 hours for the 30 percent design phase. Suppose at the end of the 30 percent phase the civil group has spent 120 hours. The PM looks at the work produced in 120 hours and determines that it is probably only 20 percent complete, not 30 percent as planned. Because 20 percent divided by 30 percent is 67 percent, the amount earned is 67 percent of 100 hours or 67 hours. The civil group took 120 hours to earn 67 hours. Should this trend continue, the civil group will spend 120 hours to accomplish or earn each additional 67 hours of work. At that rate, the civil group will have spent 600 hours, considerably more than the 400 hours planned and budgeted (see Figure 8.4).

Figure 8.5 illustrates the disparity among the civil group hours spent compared to those budgeted and earned.

Based on this analysis, the project manager should speak with the civil discipline lead and determine what is causing this disparity. Corrective action must be taken quickly. Waiting may only make the situation worse.

DETERMINING THE PERCENTAGE COMPLETE

Periodically, the earned value of the work should be checked. This is the best way to determine where the project really stands. To do so, the PM must look at the work product and

FIGURE 8.5 Civil Discipline Budget Hours

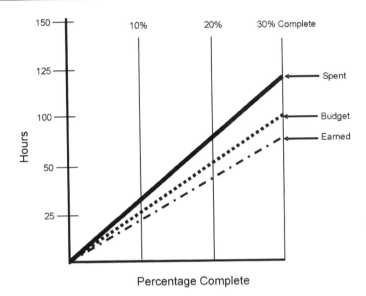

XYZ Project
CIVIL WORK – Status at 30 Percent Scheduled Completion

Graph showing the differences among the civil discipline's budgeted hours and the amount spent and earned.

judge its completion. Various techniques can be used to determine the percentages complete. All employ abduction—that is, they involve educated guessing based on experience. A technique for determining the percentage complete is described as follows.

Construction documents are made up of two primary deliverables, working drawings—sometimes called contract drawings—and specifications. It is possible to estimate their progress by comparing the work completed to the list of drawings and specifications. PMs frequently ask the discipline leads to prepare a list of drawings for the purpose of determining their fee. The list of drawings is based on the scope of work and a general understanding of how many drawings it

will take to adequately define the project for construction purposes. Generally, a list of specification sections is not prepared
for fee development purposes. The cost of writing the specifications is either factored into the hours-per-drawing figure or
a separate hour total is given by each discipline for specifications. Through experience, most disciplines know approximately how many and which specification sections will be
needed for a particular type and size of project. Once the
project starts, it is a good idea to ask the disciplines for a list of
specification sections. The list of drawings and specification
sections can be used to monitor progress. The PM can compare drawing and specification progress to these lists to get an
idea of how far along a particular discipline is.

There is no absolute way of determining the percentages
complete for drawings and specifications. PMs use different approaches. Whatever approach is used, it should not be too time
consuming or it will not be used. A relatively simple way of
checking percentage complete for drawings and specifications
is outlined here:

Drawings:

- 0%—The drawing is not started.
- 25%—The drawing has been started—plans, sections, elevations, or details are still in progress.
- 50%—Plans, sections, elevations, or details are drawn but
  not dimensioned or dimensions are missing. There are
  no notes or material call-outs or notes/callouts are incomplete or missing.
- 90%—The drawing is complete but has not been submitted for a quality-control (QC) check.
- 100%—The drawing has been checked for quality control
  and the QC comments have been corrected on the drawing.

An example is shown in Figure 8.6.

FIGURE 8.6 Construction Documents

NO.	DRAWING NO.	DRAWING TITLE	PERCENTAGE COMPLETE				
			0%	25%	50%	90%	100%
1	G-1	TITLE SHEET - CODE SUMMARY INFO		X			
2	C-1	SITE PLAN				X	
3	D-1	DEMOLITION PLAN			X		
4	A-1	FLOOR PLAN				X	
5	A-2	EXTERIOR ELEVATIONS				X	
6	A-3	BUILDING SECTIONS				X	
7	A-4	DOOR, FINISH & WINDOW SCHEDULES			X		
8	A-5	DETAILS			X		
9	S-1	FOUNDATION PLAN			X		
10	S-2	ROOF FRAMING PLAN			X		
11	S-3	DETAILS & SECTIONS			X		
12	P-1	PLUMBING PLAN			X		
13	P-2	PLUMBING DIAGRAMS & DETAILS		X			
14	FP-1	FIRE SPRINKLER PLAN			X		
15	FP-2	FIRE SPRINKLER DETAILS		X			
16	M-1	HVAC PLAN			X		
17	M-2	HVAC DETAILS			X		
18	E-1	ELECTRICAL POWER PLAN			X		
19	E-2	ELECTRICAL LIGHTING PLAN			X		
20	E-3	ELECTRICAL DETAILS AND SCHEDULES		X			
		TOTAL "Xs" PER COLUMN	0	4	12	4	0
		NUMBER OF "Xs" x PERCENT COMPLETE	0	100	600	360	0 = 1,060

1,060 (Total) / 20 (No. of Dwgs) = **53% COMPLETE**

Example showing a procedure for measuring the percentage complete of construction documents.

Specifications:

- 0%–The specification section is not started.
- 50%–The specification section has been started and is somewhere in progress.
- 90%–The specification is complete but not checked for quality control.
- 100%–The specification has been checked for quality control and the QC comments have been corrected in the specification.

Note that for specifications there is no 25 percent completion milestone. In my experience it is difficult to judge a specification as 25 percent complete because generally there is no tangible (physical) document to look at when a specification is only 25 percent complete. See Figure 8.7 for an example of measuring percent complete.

FIGURE 8.7 Construction Specifications

NO.	SPEC NO. *	SPECIFICATION TITLE	PERCENT COMPLETE			
			0%	50%	90%	100%
1	024100	DEMOLITION			X	
2	033000	CAST-IN-PLACE CONCRETE		X		
3	061000	ROUGH CARPENTRY			X	
4	062000	FINISH CARPENTRY		X		
5	072000	THERMAL INSULATION		X		
6	073113	ASPHALT SHINGLES		X		
7	076000	FLASHING & SHEET METAL			X	
8	081400	WOOD DOORS			X	
9	085200	WOOD WINDOWS		X		
10	087100	DOOR HARDWARE	X			
11	092900	GYPSUM BOARD		X		
12	096500	RESILIENT FLOORING	X			
13	099100	PAINTING	X			
14	211300	FIRE SUPPRESSION SPRINKLER SYSTEM		X		
15	220000	PLUMBING		X		
16	230000	HVAC		X		
17	260000	ELECTRICAL	X			
18	310000	EARTHWORK			X	
19	321200	PAVING			X	
		TOTAL "Xs" PER COLUMN	4	9	6	0
		NUMBER of "Xs" x PERCENT COMPLETE	0	450	540	0	990

990 (Total) / 19 (No. of Spec. Sections) = | 52% COMPLETE |

* Specification numbers are based on the Construction Specifications Institute (CSI) MasterFormat 2004 Edition.

Example showing a procedure for measuring the percentage complete of construction specifications.

COMMITMENT FROM PROJECT TEAM MEMBERS

Design team members must be willing to commit to honoring their budgets. Their buy-in is essential to the project's financial success. The PM must have a feeling of comfort that team members will earnestly try to perform within their budgets.

It is much easier to get buy-in to project budgets when design team members are asked to participate in developing their budgets in the first place. This is a major advantage of the bottom-up budget approach compared to the top-down approach. Regardless, buy-in is needed from team members, even with top-down budgets. Sometimes, it is difficult to get this buy-in from the discipline leads.

I once asked a structural engineer to commit to a budget for the structural engineering for a military training facility. This was a project where the budget was determined through negotiations and the design firm had to back down from the fee it had originally proposed. Although the structural engineer talked about many project-related issues, he would not agree or disagree to the budget. Finally, when pressed, he answered grudgingly, "Well, if you want us to work overtime for free, I suppose we could."

I thanked the engineer and decided to move the work to another engineer in another one of the firm's offices. The engineer in the other office did commit to the budget and the group performed admirably and within budget. (By the way, over the course of the next half year, other project managers had similar difficulties with the same engineer—reluctance on his part to commit to budgets. Eventually, the office manager began looking for the engineer's replacement.) Generally speaking, most design professionals will commit and honor their commitments. It is a matter of personal pride and professionalism.

A technique I have used to encourage young design professionals to commit to budgets and take responsibility for them involves the use of simple "yellow-sticky" notes. Starting with small tasks, such as designing a few details or developing the finish or door schedules, I ask them to tell me ahead of time how long they think it will take. At first, many of them are reluctant to give a specific answer. They often hedge. I remind them that the firm did not hedge when it agreed to a lump-sum or a maximum-not-to-exceed amount and that was to do the entire project. With some coaxing, they generally give an answer. If it seems too high to me, we negotiate. If it seems too low, I ask them to tell me all the steps involved or ask if they are remembering to include this or that. Usually, they come back with a higher number. When the number of hours more or less agrees with my experience, I write it down on a yellow-sticky note and stick it to his or her cubicle wall. Good naturedly, I say something like, "OK, here is the budget you agreed to; now try to live with it." Almost always they do. Many seem to appreciate the process and almost everyone learns from it. Someday, some of them will have projects of their own to manage. As PMs, they will need to learn to budget their time and the time of others. Learning early, incrementally, and in a nonthreatening manner is a painless way to learn.

THE PERILS OF PROCRASTINATION

There is a saying that numbers do not lie. Actually, they can, or at the very least, they can mislead. The following example illustrates how. On time and material (T&M) projects and even on T&M projects with maximums-not-to-exceed, design firms invoice clients (usually monthly) based on the hours spent by the firm working on the client's project. In accounting parlance, the time spent working on a project is called the actual cost of work performed (ACWP). The assumption is that the ACWP is the same as the amount that was planned to be spent to accomplish the work that was performed, or what is called the budgeted cost of work performed (BCWP). However, the ACWP does not always equal the BCWP. Sometimes the ACWP is better (cost is less) than what was planned. More often, however, it is not.

Suppose 200 hours are charged to a project in a month. Assume that the project has a T&M with a maximum-not-to-exceed contract. Assume the PM has reviewed the value of the work produced for the 200 hours and has concluded that only 150 hours were actually earned.

Should the project manager be worried? Probably, and the PM should figure out why and take corrective action so that it does not happen again. Suppose, however, the project manager is not worried, because the PM rationalizes that the project is only 50 hours behind "plan" and the 50 hours can easily be made up without making any changes to the work plan. So, the PM does nothing and the work continues. The firm invoices the client the dollar amount equivalent of 200 hours of work, the actual amount spent. The client pays the invoice.

The next month, the same thing happens, another 200 hours are spent, but according to the PM's calculations, again, only an additional 150 hours were earned. So far, after two months, a total of 400 hours have been spent, but only 300 hours have been earned. Still, the PM rationalizes (procrastinates) and does nothing. The firm invoices another 200 hours and the client pays.

The same happens the next month and the month after that and after that. The PM continues to procrastinate and does nothing. Each month the accounting department invoices the hours spent just as the T&M contract permits. The project is digging itself deeper and deeper into a hole and pulling the procrastinating PM in with it. As long as the accounting department invoices the work and the client pays the invoices, no one in accounting or upper management is the wiser. Sooner or later, however, the project will reach the maximum-not-to-exceed contract amount. When it does, the project will not be complete. Most likely it will be about 75 percent complete, based on the PM's assessments of the values earned. The design team will continue to work on and charge to the project. However, accounting will no longer be able to bill the client for the hours spent. When this happens, the PM is very likely to have upper management's attention and a lot of explaining to do. The days of procrastination will be over. There will be plenty to do and it may not be pleasant to do it! It can be very stressful for a project manager to finish a project when it is only 75 percent complete but out of money.

Project managers must look at the project work on a regular basis, determine whether the hours spent were actually earned, and take corrective action to the work plan as soon as they see a problem. This is the only way to keep little problems from turning into big ones. It is very unlikely that a problem will fix itself. The PM must do something to fix it.

Project managers must understand the accounting practices of the design firm. They must understand that in the absence of information to the contrary, most design firm accountants and upper managers assume that project managers are managing their projects properly and that the projects are advancing nicely. Most important, project managers must understand that only the PM knows the true status of the project. And the PM can only know that if he or she is paying attention to the project. It is unlikely that someone in the firm's accounting department or upper management will see a project-related problem before the project manager can and tip off the PM to the problem and suggest what to do to fix it. The project manager must read the project road signs, and safely steer the project. No backseat driver will tell the PM how to steer. After a wreck, however, plenty of backseat drivers may be telling the PM what should have been done.

By the way, had the project in the previous example been a lump-sum type project with phases such as 30 percent, 50 percent, etc., the accounting department and upper management would have probably figured out the problem sooner. If the project was over budget by the 30 percent submittal, there would be a difference between the amount of money the firm spent producing the work and the amount that the firm could invoice. The difference would equal the BCWP (in this case 30 percent of the fee) minus the ACWP. Because the ACWP is greater than the BCWP when a project is running over budget, the difference would be a negative number, which is called a negative variance. Negative variances generally attract the attention of accountants and upper management. With a lump-sum project, the project manager probably would have been asked much sooner what was going wrong with the project than in the T&M scenario described earlier. This would be to everyone's advantage, because it is much easier to fix a project when it is only 30 percent complete with money left compared to when it is 75 percent complete and out of money.

The sooner project financial problems are fixed the better, so some design firms conduct regularly scheduled project reviews. Generally, these reviews take place once a month. The formats of the reviews vary, but usually the project manager summarizes the project's design, schedule, and financial status and presents it to upper management. If the project has a problem, whether it is design, schedule, or financially related, the PM is asked to explain how he or she proposes to correct the problem. Often upper management provides suggestions. Monthly project reviews are excellent tools for detecting project problems in their infancy, when it is the easiest to fix them.

BUDGET RECOVERY STRATEGIES

Once a problem is identified, the PM must decide how to correct it. A number of strategies can be employed. Choosing the correct one depends on the specific problem and the project particulars. Here are some common problems and suggestions for fixing them:

- If one or more disciplines are doing work that was not originally planned because it was not part of the original scope of work, the work must be stopped. It is very difficult to get paid for out-of-scope work after the fact. Performing out-of-scope work is often the cause of overruns. It is a good idea to set up separate WBS codes for out-of-scope work so it can be tracked independently of the original work plan.
- If a particular discipline is running over budget on planned work and the overrun is detected early, a brief reminder to the discipline lead will usually solve the problem.
- If overruns are considerable and affect more than one discipline, it may be necessary to modify the work plan.

Sometimes it is possible to find a more effective or efficient way to perform the remainder of the work. If so, budgets can be revised to compensate for the overruns. The new work plan must be distributed to all team members. The PM needs new commitments from the team members to the new work plan and revised budgets.

- If overruns are significant, affect more than one discipline, and could prove catastrophic, it may be necessary to take drastic measures and reduce the scope of work. Generally, this is a course of last resort. Few PMs can unilaterally reduce a project's scope of work. This requires buy-in by the client. Before discussing scope reduction with the owner, the PM should consult with the firm's upper management. Because this decision may have major consequences, upper management should have a hand in making it.

CHAPTER 8 CHECKLIST

In summary, controlling the project design budget is one of the more challenging tasks that project managers face. It is also one of the most important. To survive, design firms must operate the majority of their projects on budget. Design firms expect their project managers to understand this and manage their projects' finances responsibly. To this end, project managers should ask:

- ❏ Is the design fee adequate to design the project?
- ❏ If the client says the design fee is too high, is it possible to negotiate the following: reducing the number of design alternatives, reducing the number of submittals, reducing the number of mandatory client meetings, or reducing the scope of work?
- ❏ Have I identified all the project tasks and assigned WBS codes to them?

❑ Do the tasks tie into the contract language and phase requirements?

❑ Are the WBS codes hierarchical?

❑ Is the WBS divided sufficiently to allow me to properly manage and monitor the project? Is it too complicated?

❑ Are the task names intuitive so that design team members can easily tell how to charge their time?

❑ Am I monitoring the project's financial information frequently enough to take corrective action in a timely manner?

THE NEXT CHAPTER

Another challenge that the project manager faces is the project schedule. Keeping projects on schedule involves careful planning, development of a realistic schedule, and vigilance. The next chapter discusses project scheduling.

9

PROJECT SCHEDULE CONTROL

The project schedule is an essential part of the project work plan. It is used by the project manager, the project team, the client, and the design firm's management to monitor and assess the progress of the work. Three schedule formats are commonly used. They are the milestone list, the bar chart (also called a Gantt chart), and the CPM schedule (critical path method schedule).

MILESTONE LIST SCHEDULE

The milestone list schedule, as the name suggests, is just a list, like a short grocery list, except instead of groceries it lists project milestones. Milestones are the due dates for critical or contract-defined significant activities. The list is prepared chronologically, with earlier dates and milestones listed first followed by those that logically depend on the completion of earlier milestones. For example, because preliminary design cannot start until the schematic design is complete, it comes

FIGURE 9.1   Typical Milestone List Schedule for a Design Project with Three Phases

Phase 1: Starts January 1, 2007
           Ends March 15, 2007

Phase 2: Starts April 1, 2007
           Ends September 15, 2007

Phase 3: Starts October 1, 2007
           Ends December 15, 2007

after the schematic design milestone on the list. Figure 9.1 illustrates a typical milestone list schedule.

Milestone list schedules are simple to read and understand. They are also simple to construct with standard word-processing software (even a typewriter) for they contain no graphic components. Milestone list schedules are commonly used by clients in Request for Proposals (RFQs) because they quickly convey basic project schedule information. Many small projects can be managed successfully using these milestone list schedules.

Small projects generally do not have the budgets to support the development of complex schedules. A three-week project with a budget of 80 hours, for example, does not warrant spending 16 hours to develop the project schedule. It usually takes less than an hour to develop a usable milestone list schedule for a small project.

BAR OR GANTT CHART SCHEDULE

The bar chart is the oldest graphic schedule type. As discussed in Chapter 1, it was developed in 1917 by Henry Gantt. It is by far the most common graphic type schedule because it is easy to set up and understand. For small to medium-size projects, a bar chart schedule is usually adequate to convey the necessary scheduling/milestone information to both client and team members. It also provides enough detail for the PM to effectively manage the project.

Three-week look-ahead schedules are very common in the construction industry. Superintendents of large construction projects often use simple bar chart schedules in conjunction with complex CPM schedules to manage their next three weeks of work.

A bar chart schedule has the following advantages:

- Easy to set up.
- Intuitive to read and understand by clients and team members.
- Suitable for small and medium-size projects.
- Easy to update by hand or with a computerized scheduling program.

Figure 9.2 illustrates a typical bar chart schedule.

FIGURE 9.2 Typical Format for a Bar Chart Schedule

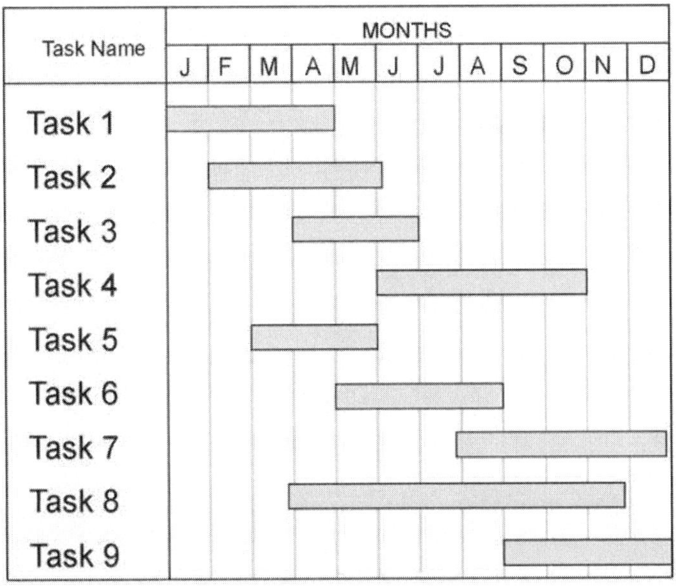

CRITICAL PATH METHOD (CPM) SCHEDULE

More complicated projects require more complicated schedules. Even though there is no magic rule, at some point, project complexity dictates using a more sophisticated project scheduling tool, such as the critical path method (CPM) schedule. Like bar chart schedules, CPM schedules may be set up originally by hand on graph paper, but usually they are developed using one of many software computer programs. The CPM is a process flow diagram superimposed on a timeline. Project tasks are laid out chronologically and in the proper order of execution.

Critical path method schedules are so named because they graphically show the flow of work through the schedule where there is no slack time or float. Any task along this path is deemed "critical" because if it takes longer to complete the task than was originally planned the overall project schedule invariably slips. Figure 9.3 illustrates a typical CPM schedule.

FIGURE 9.3   Typical CPM Schedule Showing Critical Path

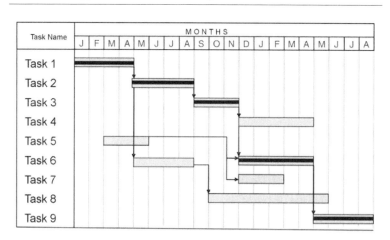

Computer-generated CPM schedules have a number of advantages:

- Are suitable for larger projects with numerous tasks.
- Interdependencies among tasks are shown.
- Tasks can have attributes: start and finish dates, durations, predecessors, successors, and labor-hour budgets.
- Once set up, the computer program determines the project's critical path.
- If tasks slip, their new end dates can be entered into the program and the program can recalculate the critical path and/or determine the project's new end date.

SELECTING A PROJECT SCHEDULING METHOD

Scheduling simple and more complicated design projects usually start the same way, with a milestone list schedule. If the design project is a simple one, a milestone list schedule may be all that is required for the team, client, and the PM's project management purposes. If the design project is too complicated for a milestone list schedule to convey the information and/or the level of detail required, then the next schedule choice is the bar chart schedule. If the design project is large with dozens of tasks and numerous submittals, a computer-generated CPM schedule is probably necessary.

Like project planning activities, schedules are built iteratively. They start simply but are all encompassing. More and more detail is then added within the basic framework. While schedules may be generated using computers, the computer cannot plan the schedule; it can only assist in drawing it and keeping it current. The specific logic and needs of a project schedule are up to the project manager. The scheduling information, task interdependencies, and deliverable milestone dates drive the requirements and complexity of the schedule. The computer program cannot determine any of this on its own.

MILESTONES

Two types of project milestones exist—the contractual milestones that are required by the agreement between the design professional and the owner (major milestones) and the additional milestones that the project manager uses to plan, execute, and monitor the work of the design team (minor milestones).

When building either a bar chart or a CPM schedule, start by identifying the major milestones required by the agreement for these are the fundamental contract requirements that must be met. It is also wise to use the same milestone terminology that is contained in the agreement. For example, most design projects contain phases that are defined in the agreement. Using the same phase terminology in the schedule makes it easier to keep track of how the project is progressing in relation to the contract requirements.

Many years ago, the American Institute of Architects (AIA) used specific names for the phase designations in its document B141, Standard Form of Agreement Between Owner and Architect. The phases were: schematic design, design development, and construction documents. However, document B141 now gives the owner and architect more flexibility in defining project phases. In effect, architects and owners can call the phases anything they choose. But the schematic design, design development, and construction documents phases are still commonly used.

Many engineering projects use percentages complete to indicate phases such as 15 percent, 50 percent, 90 percent, and 100 percent, instead of phase names. Percentage designations vary depending on many factors, but the idea is the same—the overall project is broken down into contractually defined major milestones with specific deliverable requirements.

Many federal agencies divide the design phase into two major parts called Title I and Title II services. Title I services relate to schematic design and design development phases, more or less, while Title II services relate to the construction documents phase. Title III services are services during construction. Sometimes Title II services are further subdivided by the agreement into percentages of completion. For example, 75 percent complete and 100 percent complete are two very common percentages used on relatively small Title II services agreements.

Agreements include a due date to indicate when the project is supposed to be completed. These dates can be expressed as specific dates, such as December 31, 2006, or as a number of weeks (4 weeks) or calendar days (250 calendar days). Weeks and calendar days are generally measured from the Notice to Proceed (NPS). The NPS is the date when written authorization is given by the owner instructing the design firm to begin work.

The schedule is built by first drawing the major milestones as vertical lines on a horizontal timeline. Figures 9.4 and 9.5 illustrate typical major contract milestones for two contracts that use different terminology.

FIGURE 9.4 Project Schedule

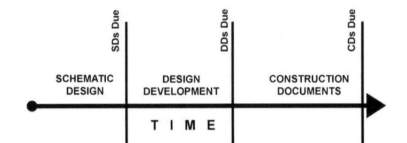

A project schedule begins by dividing the overall project into its contractual phases. The contractual phase due dates become the schedule's "contract milestones" or "major milestones."

FIGURE 9.5   Another Project Schedule

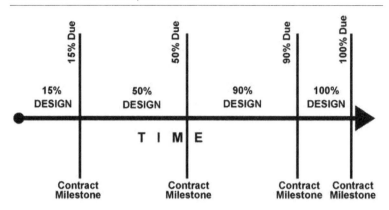

As in Figure 9.4, the schedule begins by dividing the overall project into its contractual phases. Here the contract uses different terminology so the schedule does, too.

The next step is to identify minor milestones. Minor milestones are the steps along the way, the dates when tasks must be completed to reach the major milestone dates on time. For example, to complete a schematic design, it may be necessary to perform a program validation exercise, make a topographic survey of the project site, and prepare a geotechnical report, as shown in Figure 9.6.

To be as useful as possible, the minor milestones dates should be spread out more or less evenly throughout the phase, not grouped together at the beginning or end, which will defeat their purpose. Minor milestones are like mileposts along the road—it is much easier to judge the speed one is going when mileposts are regularly spaced.

The next step is to add task bars. Remember that a task has an objective, duration, and a level of effort. In addition, a task has a relationship with other tasks, tasks on which it is dependent and tasks which depend on it. The schedule graphically shows task durations and interdependencies. Because design professionals are visual people by nature, a schedule can quickly convey a lot of information to design team members.

FIGURE 9.6   Minor Milestones

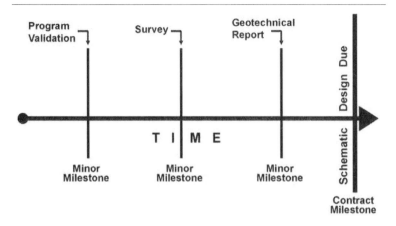

Schedule for the schematic design phase showing minor milestones spread more or less evenly throughout the phase.

Every task bar has a name designation, a start date, and a finish date. Task bars are laid out chronologically in relation to each other. The length of the bar between its start date and finish date graphically illustrates the task's duration. See Figure 9.7.

These are the basics of a bar chart schedule: a horizontal timeline, vertical major and minor milestones, and task bars.

PASS-THE-BATON AND PARALLEL SCHEDULING

In Figure 9.7, one task ends before the next task begins. This technique of task scheduling is sometimes called "pass-the-baton" scheduling. In pass-the-baton scheduling, one task finishes its run and then its information (or deliverable) is passed to the next task, like runners in a relay race passing the baton from one to another. In scheduling parlance, the technique is called "finish-to-start" (FS)—one task finishes before the next task starts.

FIGURE 9.7 More Minor Milestones

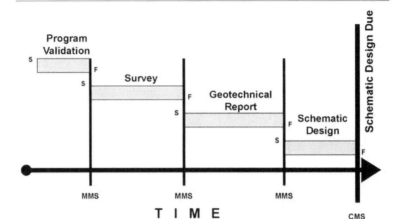

Schedule for the schematic design of a hypothetical project showing tasks and "minor milestones."

Often, there is a faster way to accomplish the work and, therefore, improve schedule performance. Tasks can run in parallel and tasks can have overlapping finish and start dates.

The trick to improving schedule performance is to know which tasks can overlap, which ones can run in parallel, and which must finish before other tasks can start. For example, the detailed design of a three-story building's heating, ventilating, and air-conditioning (HVAC) system should not start until the floor plans and building envelope (walls, roof, and window area) are determined, because these affect the building's heat loss and heat gain, which, in turn, affect the sizing of HVAC equipment and duct runs. If the floor plan and exterior elevations are subject to significant changes, premature work on the HVAC design will likely have to be done over again. Project managers must plan the design work to minimize rework as much as possible. To avoid rework, certain tasks should not begin until other tasks are complete.

Contractually, some tasks cannot start without client approval and the client issuing the NTP for the next phase. For example, the agreement may stipulate that the construction documents phase cannot start until the client has reviewed and approved the design development deliverables and has issued a notice to proceed. It is important to know what the agreement says. As already discussed in Chapter 6, it is not a good idea to start work until authorized to do so. Should the client pull the plug for some reason, the design firm may not get paid for the work it was not authorized to perform.

Tasks that do not rely on information from each other can run in parallel, i.e., run concurrently. For instance, during the construction documents phase, the tasks of preparing and drawing the door, window, and finish schedules can be run in parallel. Other tasks are interrelated, requiring frequent coordination and/or input from each other. Tasks such as these benefit from concurrent planning. The design of a building's suspended acoustical ceiling, for example, requires input from multiple disciplines: architecture, mechanical, and electrical (and fire protection if the building has a fire-suppression system). The architect develops the overall reflected ceiling plan, but input is needed from the mechanical and electrical engineers. Coordination among the disciplines is necessary so that room lighting is adequate, spaces are conditioned properly, and the desired overall aesthetic effect is achieved. Lighting fixtures must avoid interference with HVAC ductwork and vice versa. Ceiling air diffusers and return-air grilles must be laid out to optimize conditioned air distribution but not interfere with light fixtures. Lighting must be laid out to achieve the footcandle levels required for the proper functional use of the room but not interfere with ceiling diffusers and return-air grilles. Each discipline must understand and respect the needs and concerns of the others. Because frequent feedback and communication among the three is needed for all three designs to proceed efficiently, running the three tasks concurrently—in parallel—makes sense.

Tasks can overlap in different ways. Some tasks require input from other tasks but do not necessarily have to wait until the other task is fully complete. For example, the schematic design of a building may need preliminary site information from a surveyor before proceeding, but not necessarily the final survey. A geotechnical investigation needs some survey information before it can proceed and it needs a general idea of the building location before field drilling can begin. In situations like this, the tasks can overlap. Figure 9.8 illustrates a schematic design phase where these tasks overlap.

Note that in Figure 9.8 the survey begins at the same time as the program validation task. These two tasks can run in parallel because they do not rely on each other for input.

FIGURE 9.8 Parallel Tasks

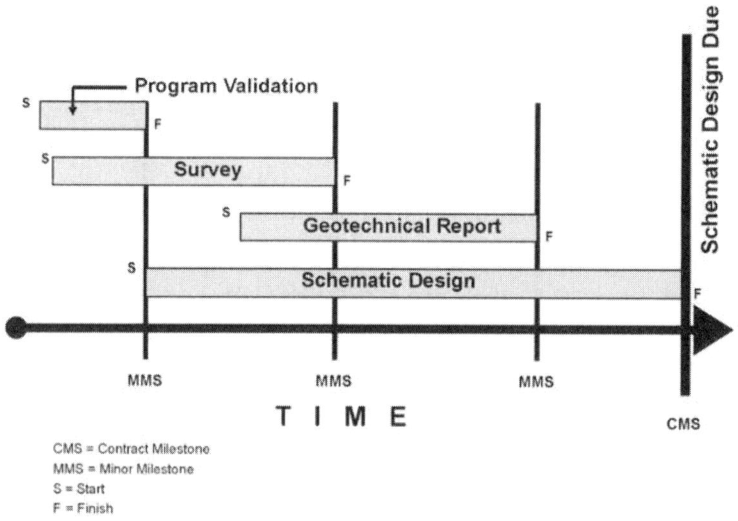

Schedule for a schematic design showing tasks running in parallel instead of concurrently as in Figure 9.7.

SCHEDULING JARGON

In scheduling parlance, the first task in an FS (finish-to-start) relationship is called the *predecessor*. The second task is called the *successor*. Predecessor and successor tasks can be related in ways other than FS (finish-to-start). They can relate:

- Start-to-start (SS)—tasks are interrelated and start at the same time.
- Start-to-finish (SF)—tasks are interrelated and one task finishes when the other one starts.
- Finish-to-finish (FF)—tasks are interrelated and finish at the same time.

There can also be a time delay between tasks. This delay is called lag. For example, suppose Task A takes 14 days to complete. Task B requires input from Task A when it is approximately 50 percent complete but it does not require Task A to be complete before Task B starts. Task A and Task B can be scheduled with a start-to-start relationship with a lag of seven days for the start of Task B.

Figure 9.9 illustrates the various ways predecessor and successor tasks can relate to each other.

CPM SCHEDULING

The critical path method of scheduling uses the relationship terms described previously and illustrated in Figure 9.8. It uses relationship arrows showing dependencies among the tasks. Depending on the configuration of the arrow, slack time in the schedule is shown graphically. In addition, a CPM schedule highlights the path through the tasks where there is no float. Figure 9.10 converts the bar chart schedule shown in Figure 9.8 into a CPM schedule.

FIGURE 9.9   The Four Scheduling Relationships of Tasks

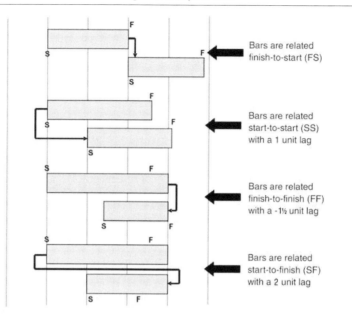

FIGURE 9.10   A Typical CPM Schedule Showing Tasks and Tasks Predecessors

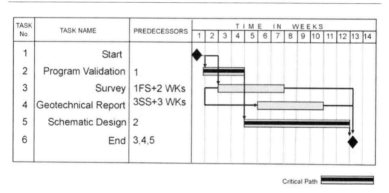

Note how the CPM schedule conveys more information than does the bar chart schedule. It illustrates that the schematic design depends on the completion of the program validation. Note, too, how the CPM schedule shows the time lag

between the start of the survey and the start of the geotechnical report. Remember that the geotechnical investigation requires some input from the survey task before it can begin, thus the time lag before it starts. The schematic design deliverables cannot be completed until the program validation, survey, geotechnical report, and schematic design are complete, because they are predecessors to the schematic design submittal.

USEFUL SCHEDULING

These are the basics for preparing a project schedule. How useful the schedule is depends on how much planning and thought goes into making it. If it is approached as a required abstract assignment and not as a planning tool, then its usefulness will be limited. To be a useful planning tool, the schedule needs to address the following:

- Show all contractually required phases as major milestones. If the schedule will be reproduced in color, consider showing these in red so they will not be confused with minor milestones that can change.
- Show minor milestones to give the project mileposts—regular intervals of time where progress can be monitored.
- Show all tasks required to complete the deliverables for the major milestones. Use a level of detail appropriate for the size and complexity of the project.
- Make sure quality control/review is a budgeted task.
- Show client review periods as tasks.

METHODS FOR SHORTENING SCHEDULES

Sometimes project schedules must be shortened. A number of decisions can be revisited to shorten a project schedule. In the construction industry, one of the first places to look is overtime. Working more hours in a day usually means the work will take fewer days to complete. This is an option for design firms as well. Of course, doing so usually increases the project costs. In addition, overtime is generally only a short-term option. Planning to work overtime over a period of many weeks or months is a bad idea. Efficiency and accuracy tend to drop off after many weeks of constant overtime.

Before looking at overtime to solve the problem, the following options are worth considering:

- *Shorten task contingencies.* Contingency time is frequently built into many tasks. For example, the structural engineer might tell the PM that the structural discipline needs four weeks to design the foundation, when really it can be completed in three. The structural engineer has padded the task time because this gives him or her more flexibility in managing the work of this particular project in relation to the other work his or her department may have. It is worth speaking to the structural engineer again to explain the scheduling problem. Team members are generally cooperative; if they think they can shorten the time they need, they will.
- *Run tasks concurrently (in parallel).* Can some tasks that are running sequentially be run at the same time?
- *Shorten client reviews.* Can the client take less time to review and approve the submittals?
- *Use more resources.* Can the design firm commit more resources to the project and therefore complete some tasks more quickly? One word of caution, however: if people start working on the project who are not familiar with it, a learning curve may dig into the budget.
- *Extend the due date.* Can the client grant a time extension? Projects are frequently due on a Friday by the end of the day. This means that printing and assembling the deliverables has to take place by the end of the day Thursday or first thing Friday morning. If the client will accept the

project Monday morning, it may make no difference to the client but it will give the project team the weekend to work. Sometimes all that is needed is another couple of days.

CHAPTER 9 CHECKLIST

Three types of schedules are commonly used by design professionals: milestone list, bar chart (Gantt chart), and critical path method (CPM). The project manager should consider the following when setting up the schedule and monitoring the project schedule.

- ❐ Did I choose the appropriate type of schedule for the project?
  - Milestone list—simple projects with short schedules and few tasks
  - Bar chart—moderately sized and moderately complex projects with no more than a dozen or two tasks
  - CPM—complicated projects with multiple phases and numerous tasks
- ❐ Does the contract stipulate the type of project schedule? If so, am I using it?
- ❐ Is there sufficient detail in the schedule so I can properly manage and monitor project progress?
- ❐ Does the schedule use the same project phase names and task terminology as are used in the contract?
- ❐ Does the schedule have major milestone due dates that agree with the contract-required due dates?
- ❐ Have I scheduled sufficient time for quality-control reviews prior to each submittal?
- ❐ Have I scheduled enough time for client reviews?

Sometimes it is necessary to shorten a project's schedule. To shorten project duration, the PM should consider the following:

❐ Can I run some tasks in parallel?

❐ Can some successor tasks start before predecessor tasks are 100 percent complete?

❐ Are time contingencies built into some of the tasks? If so, can these be reduced?

❐ Can client review periods be shortened?

❐ Would the addition of more staff shorten the time needed to perform certain tasks?

❐ Can the client grant a time extension?

THE NEXT CHAPTER

In addition to managing the project schedule, risk, and budget, the project manager must also manage the design team. The next chapter looks at this important project management responsibility.

10

PROJECT TEAM MANAGEMENT

In his book *Synagoge,* the fourth-century Roman historian Pappus of Alexandria recounted Archimedes's excitement upon inventing the lever. "Give me a place to stand and I will move the earth," he quoted Archimedes as proclaiming.[42]

A project manager's job is not to move the world, of course, although at times it may seem as daunting. The PM's job is to move the design team, and move it in such a way that it successfully completes the project. To do so, the project manager must employ leverage to make the design team strong enough to accomplish the task. Basically, there are two ways of leveraging a design team: (1) harness the team and drive it forward or (2) unleash it, thus empowering it to develop its own synergetic power. The latter is much more effective.

FIGURE 10.1   Twenty-Mule Team

Photograph courtesy of U.S. Borax.

THE HARNESSED DESIGN TEAM

In the Southern Californian desert between 1883 and 1889, 20-mule teams hauled borax ore 160 miles from Death Valley to the railroad junction at Mohave (see Figure 10.1). Twenty mules were harnessed to three wagons, two loaded with ore while the third held a large tank with a 16-day supply of water. With a full water supply, the three wagons weighed a staggering 37 tons! A little arithmetic yields the astounding fact that a single mule can pull 3,700 pounds!

While the strength of the mule team is impressive, the truth about a mule team is that it is only as strong as the sum of the mules. Each mule has more or less the same capability. A few may be able to pull a bit more than others, but that is basically it. Mules are beasts of burden. When harnessed together, simple arithmetic determines the team's overall brute strength.

Some design teams are built this way, too. The team is banded together for a particular project and driven by the project manager. The problem, of course, is that design professionals are not mules. Design professionals differ tremendously from one another, with various skills and experience. A design team needs multidisciplinary professionals with various capabilities who perform different functions and produce different deliverables, some of which must logically trail others. Lashing the design team together and driving them forward as if they will or should pull together is foolhardy.

A few years ago I had an opportunity to watch a project manager self-destruct. A tightly wired, inexperienced, and autocratic-type PM, with little patience for the opinions of others, ran his project in a manner that Machiavelli and any mule driver would have appreciated. The project had a very tight schedule and budget. He gave orders that sounded much like commandments filled with "shalls" and "shall nots." "This shall be done by x date." "You shall not spend more than 16 hours to complete task X, period." "You department heads will stamp and sign your drawings by Friday or else!" As it turned out, his project went over budget and finished behind schedule.

The fact that the project turned out poorly is not hard to understand. The PM did nothing to actually encourage, facilitate, or empower the team to perform within the constraints of the tight budget and schedule. Instead, he harnessed them with edicts and threats. He achieved the opposite effect that he intended. He discouraged, dissuaded, and dampened team enthusiasm—he disabled the team. Harnessed design teams tend to chomp at the bit.

Take, for example, the PM's threat, "You department heads will stamp and sign your drawings by Friday or else!" Licensed design professionals take their state licensures very seriously, more seriously than any threat suggesting that they misuse it. Competent department heads are not reckless nor cavalier with their registration stamps. Most will not stamp or sign drawings until they are certain that the drawings are complete, checked, and ready to be stamped. State licensure boards expect this behavior and state laws require it. Ordering department heads to stamp drawings by a specific date whether the drawings are finished or not is likely to make them bristle. It is even more likely to draw their ire if the PM is a difficult person to work for (notice the words *work for* and not *work with*).

The project manager's harnessed-team approach to team management was counterproductive. It created resentment and dissension. Alienated team members are not likely to put in the extra effort and overtime (for which they often are not paid) to complete a project on time.

When the schedule was not met, it was time for the project manager to enact his "or else." Of course, there was no "or else." Few project managers have the authority to fire someone in a matrix organization (see Chapter 3). They can, of course, ask a department head to remove a person from their project. Removing a team member from the team, however, does not always benefit the project or the project manager. It only benefits the lucky employee who no longer has to work on a floundering project for a belligerent PM. Because department heads are not subordinate to PMs in a matrix organization, the PM's threats were only roars of a paper lion. Paper lions make lousy project managers.

When the PM could not fire anybody, he did the only thing he could think of—actually, he probably did it without thinking. Hopping mad, he roared and swore at a department head in front of other employees. He kicked a partition, bending it pretty badly. Needless to say, this did not help finish the project, but it did finish the project manager.

In hindsight, it was a mistake for the firm to have made this particular individual a project manager. He did not have—to use Tom Wolfe's phrase—"the right stuff." His experience had been in business development before he was made a project manager, but he did not have the required skills and temperament needed to lead a design team. Just because someone is good at one thing does not mean that person will be good at something else. Dr. Laurence J. Peter pointed this out in his now famous 1969 book, *The Peter Principle*:

> In time, every post tends to be occupied by an employee who is incompetent to carry out its duties.[43]

THE EMPOWERED DESIGN TEAM

Project managers must be enablers not disablers. It is not the individual control of the project manager that makes a design team most successful. It is the ability of the project manager to empower the design team. In their popular book *Empowering Employees,* management consultants Kenneth L. Murrell and Mimi Meredith wrote:

> In an empowering organization [such as a design team], power becomes less about one person controlling another and more about the capacity within every person to create, develop, and distribute power to accomplish individual and shared goals.[44]

Although it may sound like faulty arithmetic, an empowered design team is actually stronger than the sum of its individual members, because an empowered team is leveraged to create its own synergy.

Remember the discussion of synergy with social scientist Mary Parker Follett from Chapter 1. In *The New State*, she wrote, ". . . problems can be solved, not . . . by mechanical aggregations, but by the subtle process of the intermingling of all the different ideas of the group."[45] Although she did not use the word, she described synergy. Team synergy is the phenomenon by which the combination of individuals with different skills, working together, with the freedom to express their ideas, produces results that are geometrically better than the sum of what they could achieve individually.

In his book *The Human Organization,* Rensis Likert, professor of psychology and sociology, wrote of the importance to an organization of bringing out the best in its employees. This applies equally well to project managers who need to bring out the best in their design teams:

> . . . the performance and output of any enterprise depend entirely upon the quality of the human organization and its capacity to function as a tightly knit, highly motivated, technically competent entity, i.e., as a highly effective interaction-influence system . . . Successful organizations are those making the best use of competent personnel to perform well and efficiently all the tasks required by the enterprise.[46]

PMs who empower team members create a project work environment that results in an interactive synergetic team of highly motivated design professionals. Empowered teams rise to the challenges of the project and resolve them.

CREATING AN EMPOWERED SYNERGETIC TEAM

Creating a synergetic team is not so difficult as it may sound. It requires the combination of project planning and project management skills already discussed in previous chapters. To manage the project, the PM must effectively facilitate and release the creative powers of the team members. Murrell and Meredith pointed out that the act of empowering a team accomplishes six important team-building objectives simultaneously. "Empowering informs, leads, coaches, serves, creates and liberates."[47] Together, these team-building objectives

contribute to developing team synergy. Synergetic teams require the following levers:

- A clearly defined project scope of work
- Clearly defined roles, responsibilities, and obligations
  for team members
- A clearly defined work plan
- Delegation of technical decisions to the right team mem-
  ber(s) while the PM retains all decision-making responsi-
  bility regarding scope, budget, and schedule
- Team buy-in to the work plan
- A clear demarcation line between iterative design and
  linear production

The last three levers require a bit more explanation.

DELEGATION OF TECHNICAL DECISIONS

Empowering a design team requires the delegation of certain project decisions to various design team members. Decisions regarding the overall project's scope of work, budget,
and schedule cannot be delegated. These decisions must reside with the project manager or the PM will lose control of
three of the important goals of project management for which
he or she is personally responsible: meeting project objectives,
meeting them on budget, and meeting them on time. But technical decisions can and should be delegated. For example, the
structural design of a building foundation and the decisions
associated with its design should be delegated to the structural
engineer. In addition to the structural design, the structural
engineer should also be responsible for managing the structural budget. The structural engineer must also be responsible
for coordinating the structural work with the other disciplines. The same goes for the mechanical, electrical, civil engineers, etc. Each discipline must know that it is accountable

Project Management for Design Professionals

for the design and decisions relevant to that discipline and the coordination of that discipline with the other disciplines. Also, each discipline must know and be responsible for managing its budget.

Sometimes there is a no-man's-land between disciplines. For example, the extent of the mechanical and civil engineers' responsibilities outside of a building are often unclear. Which engineer is responsible for which utilities can vary, depending on project circumstances. The PM must recognize that some interfaces between disciplines are muddy and that it is the PM's responsibility to make sure that these areas are defined early in the project.

Members of an empowered team know what their own responsibilities are, what the responsibilities of other team members are, and who is responsible for coordination of the work. An empowered team knows what decisions can be made among team members and what decisions must be made by the PM. Empowered team members know what their hour budgets are, what submittal they are working toward, when the submittal is due, and what deliverables are expected.

The PM of an empowered team is not a hands-off project manager. A hands-off project manager "hopes" that team members live up to their responsibilities and sits back with fingers crossed. An empowering project manager stays in the middle, coaches and oversees the design, leads the team, and attends to their needs so that everyone has what they need to meet their obligations.

If an empowered team member begins to struggle, the empowering PM tries to determine why. Perhaps directions were unclear or maybe something unexpected happened. Maybe other PMs have been vying for the team member's time. Maybe the team member is a bit unorganized or having difficulty making a decision. Whatever the reason, an empowering PM does not ignore the problem. Instead, the PM inquires, coaches, encourages, and assists. An empowering PM does not scold someone for poor performance. An empowering PM never ridicules a person in front of others. If there is a recurring problem that requires a heart-to-heart conversation, it must take place privately.

TEAM BUY-IN TO THE WORK PLAN

Although the project manager is responsible for the project work plan, the PM needs a commitment from the design team that they accept the work plan, budget, and schedule and that they will meet their various project obligations. In addition, for some projects—generally the higher-profile ones—the PM may need buy-in from the design firm's upper management and from the client as well. Buy-in is often easier if key team members have some say in developing the project work plan.

A technique that has been used successfully for many decades is the wall chart. A large conference room—some firms call it the "war room"—with a large white board, tackboard, or enough wall space to hang very large sheets of paper is used. All key team members attend a work-planning session. The session is usually led by the project manager or by a firm principal, or someone else in the firm with experience in project planning and scheduling. I once participated in a session that was led by an outside facilitator and attended by the client and a firm principal.

Before arriving, the key team members should review the project scope of work. The room's tackboard, white board, or large pieces of paper are prepared with grid lines. Vertical grid lines represent blocks of time, weeks, months, or years, depending on which is most useful for the particular project. The horizontal lines are boundary lines for tasks or disciplines. For example, if a project requires an architect, landscape architect, civil, structural, mechanical, and electrical engineer, then these are listed along the left side of the grid.

Contractual major milestone dates are added as heavy vertical lines. Sometimes, colored tape or colored yarn is used so that it is easier to move the milestone dates if necessary. Additional milestone dates can be added using different colored tape or yarn. For instance, the transition between iterative design and linear production, as discussed in Chapter 5, is a key milestone. There will be more to say about this important juncture shortly.

Using 3×5-inch cards, the team works together to build the schedule. I recall one session where each discipline was given different colored cards to use. The team collaboratively determines the tasks required. The tasks are written on the cards and tacked or taped to the grid in proper relationship to the vertical timelines and the horizontal task/discipline lines, and in the proper relationship to one another. This usually takes several attempts before all the proper relationships are figured out.

The process employs pragmatic abduction, educated guessing based on expertise, and experience as discussed previously. Lines are drawn between tasks that depend on one another, employing the line, arrow, and scheduling terms discussed in Chapter 9.

As the work session proceeds, scheduling conflicts and information needs among team members can be addressed right on the spot. Team members can explain what information they need to get started with their tasks, and estimate how long they will take. Because the cards are taped or tacked, they can be easily moved around. Everyone can see how their work relates to the whole and how it affects the work of others. The wall chart empowers a project team because it involves the team members in a mutually cooperative way with the project's work plan right from the beginning of the project.

Once all the tasks on the wall chart are arranged in the proper relation to one another, the project's critical path can be determined by drawing a red line through all the tasks that have no float in them. Once everyone agrees to the work plan, the PM can be confident that there is buy-in to the work plan because everyone had a say in building it.

A CLEAR DEMARCATION LINE BETWEEN ITERATIVE DESIGN AND LINEAR PRODUCTION

At a point in the design of a project, a shift in the approach occurs. At the beginning of the project, the iterative, holistic approach is dominant. This is the typical designer's approach: to look at the big picture while developing overall designs that address all the project design parameters. As more and more portions of the project are fleshed out—usually near the end of the preliminary design—the iterative approach gives way to a more linear, technical problem-solving approach. By the time the project is in the throes of construction documents, the approach is fundamentally linear.

Authors C. Gray, W. P. Hughes, and J. Bennett argued in their book, *The Successful Management of Design: A Handbook of Building Design Management,* that PMs should shift their projects as quickly as possible from the iterative approach to the linear approach to increase the likelihood of the project's success.[48] Kenneth Allinson explained the Gray, Hughes, and Bennett approach this way:

> This amounts to a concept of dominance shift: a management of the project so that, as room for maneuver becomes constrained during project development, project efforts are increasingly dominated by "practical men" . . . The intention is to marginalize the designer's [iterative approach's] influence.[49]

When a project moves from an iterative approach to linear depends on the project. The speed of the handoff is not so important as its quality. Before the approach changes from iterative to linear, all major parts of the project should be defined and they should meet the client's functional, technical, aesthetic, and financial objectives and expectations. If the project is well defined before the linear production of construction

documents begins, the likelihood of the project ending successfully is very high.

On the other hand, if the design is not complete and still
evolving, then changes are likely to occur during the linear production phase. Also, if designers keep designing, exploring
other alternatives and implementing them because they feel
they are better than previous solutions, additional changes will
occur.

It can be very expensive to make changes during the production of construction documents. Construction drawings
are interrelated—changes made to one often affect many other
sheets. Rework can consume considerable time and zap team
enthusiasm. A once-empowered team quickly becomes less and
less empowered with each change. Tension or frustration can
lead to friction among team members. A world-famous example will drive home this point. The Sydney Opera House is a
textbook example of how not to execute the design process for
a building.

The winning entry for the 1957 international competition
for the design of the Sydney Opera House was submitted by
the Danish architect Jørn Utzon (b. 1918). Utzon's design was
a series of diagrammatic sketches depicting pointed-arched
shells interlocking in a graceful and dramatic way, reminiscent
of the sails of a colossal 19th-century sailing ship.

Of the more than 200 entries, Utzon's sketches stood out,
captivating the competition's selection committee. Certain
that the sketches could be developed into one of world's greatest buildings, the committee selected Utzon's design.

An estimate at the time concluded it would cost about $5.6
million (U.S. dollars) to construct Utzon's design. A project
schedule was developed, setting completion of construction by
the end of 1962, with the Opera House's grand opening near
the beginning of 1963.

A design team was assembled to assist Utzon, and the challenge of turning his loosely defined sketches into a constructable building began. In addition to Utzon, the team included

mechanical, electrical, heating and ventilating, lighting, and acoustical engineers. It also included the London-based structural engineering firm of Ove Arup (1895–1988), renowned for his work with thin-shell structures. The project had no project manager per se. Utzon and Arup were coequals or co-principals of sorts. Utzon was responsible for the architectural design, Arup for the structural design and, through a number of subcontracts, for the other engineering disciplines as well. The client, New South Wales, established a part-time executive committee to provide project oversight. The committee was a political body, however, without the technical expertise needed to appreciate the coordination complexities inherent in directing a multinational design team working from their various offices throughout the world. By January of 1959, the design team was busy at work.

While buildings are constructed from the ground up, their structural systems are designed from the roof down. Nevertheless, before a satisfactory solution for the building roof structure was complete, the foundation design was under way. Utzon and the acoustical engineer had not yet resolved the building's acoustical problems. Also, Utzon was still designing the seating arrangement and struggling with the stage and backstage scenery areas. In addition, the client was still refining its ideas about the Opera House overall and making changes. Although everyone was still designing, construction drawings for the foundation were being developed. Even more amazing, however, arrangements were being made to begin construction!

Although the design of the Opera House was still in a major state of flux, a contract for construction of its foundation was let in January of 1959. Construction began while Arup was still figuring out how to structurally support the building. Many alternative schemes had been explored and discarded. A particularly nasty problem was the building's resistance to wind. The building was a series of sails, and sails are the shape they are to propel ships. Opera houses, on the other hand, are not supposed to move in the wind. The building's sail-like geometry was working at cross-purposes with the needs of a stationary building.

The building's reinforced concrete foundation was completed in 1961. In 1962, Arup completed the roof design. In 1963, instead of the planned grand opening, major portions of the foundation were demolished to construct new foundations to support the final roof design. Matters worsened. The relationship between the coprincipals began to fray. Soon Utzon refused to talk with and take direction from Arup. In 1965, the government of New South Wales took payment responsibilities away from the oversight committee and it stopped paying Utzon. In February of 1966 Utzon resigned from the project.

The Sydney Opera House was finally completed in 1973, ten years behind schedule. Despite its tumultuous design process, it stands today as one of the world's greatest architectural marvels. It is as synonymous with Sydney as the Eiffel Tower is with Paris and the Statue of Liberty with New York City. The cost overrun of the Opera House is a world marvel, too. Instead of the $5.6 million originally estimated, the Sydney Opera House cost $81.6 million, an astounding 1,450 percent cost overrun!

There is a lesson in the Sydney Opera House design process for project managers: Do not let production work get ahead of design work. True, in the case of the Sydney Opera House, this problem was exacerbated because construction work began too soon as well. Nevertheless, the lesson is clear: Major building design components that affect the overall size and arrangement of the building and affect interdisciplinary design work must be determined and fixed before linear production work begins. This also applies to the process of planning the work: Think through and establish the work plan before beginning the actual work. Herein lies the importance of the wall chart as discussed previously. This is a planning tool that allows the project manager to work with the design team to develop an effective work plan that is agreeable to everyone.

A TEAM MANAGEMENT STORY

Many years ago, I attended a very unusual job interview. The project was for a large port facility in Southern California. The interview was very different, because it included a test. I was proposed to be the PM for the project. The design team and I were given a mock project and asked to develop a schematic design right there on the spot in 45 minutes. The client explained the project and handed out a site plan and a building program of spaces. While the test caught me off guard, I was especially surprised when the client's representatives took seats at the back of the room to watch the process!

Each of us spent five minutes reading the program. During this time I made a decision: If the port wants to watch us work, we will work out loud. I enabled the team to take part in the mock design by making it very clear to my teammates exactly what they were supposed to do. I quickly broke the project into basic design components based on discipline and called out specific design assignments to each team member. This empowered the discipline members to contribute to the solution within their areas of expertise. It also gave them a degree of comfort so they could "act" appropriately within the artificial environment that was thrust upon us. For example, the civil engineer was given site development and asked to evaluate alternative locations for the main site entrance and to develop parking alternatives.

For the next 20 minutes or so, we worked this way, with discipline leads calling out their discoveries. I listened and asked follow-up questions. "What about this? Did you try that?" For the last 20 minutes, we worked together to combine the design components, talked through the problems, and integrated the solutions while I drew like crazy.

Somehow, we managed to win the project, and because we did I had the opportunity to find out why the client conducted the interview as it did. A port official claimed that in her experience the success of a design project hinges on how well the

PM takes charge, communicates, and works with the design team and not on which team has better qualified team members. What the port was looking for, she said, was a project manager who would lead and empower the design team to work together as a team because this would produce the better project. In her opinion, a strong project manager who empowers the design team almost guarantees a successful project, while a strong team with a weak PM who does not empower the team generally means the opposite will occur.

OFFSHORING

Rome—and everything else in the world—was not built in a day. But, up until recently, it was designed and built without computers. Then everything changed. During the late 1980s and early 1990s, the design professions experienced a major transformation. Design firms moved away from drawing by hand to drawing by computer. The struggle was arduous. Design firms scrambled to learn as much as they could about Computer Aided Design and Drafting (CADD) systems. In the 1980s, they spent large sums of money buying computers, peripheral hardware, and software—everything necessary to draw by computer. They hired people who knew how to keep the computers and software running and they began training their employees how to use them. Drawings that used to take 40 hours to draw by hand now took 60 hours or more. Instead of untaping drawings from drafting boards in a matter of minutes and sending them out for printing, drawings were plotted in-house, a process that took half a day or longer, assuming the plotter worked and the drawings looked like they were supposed to when plotted.

Many firms, exasperated, actually finished drawings by hand, because they could not afford to finish them by computer. Some firms ran night shifts, red-marking drawings during the day while the computer drafting "techies" drew them and plotted them, staring at and fussing with computers and plotters all night long. Everyone struggled.

But today, the problems have been sorted out and computer drafting is the norm. The bugs (most of them anyway) have been worked out and CADD is accepted and expected by all. CADD has many advantages over hand drawings. It is generally easier to make changes to drawings, particularly those changes that affect multiple disciplines. Most design firms have computerized libraries of standardized details that can be easily modified by computer and used on project after project. Today, virtually all construction documents are produced using one form of CADD program or another. Computers have affected architectural design as well. Contemporary architects such as Peter Eisenman and Frank Gehry use computers to deliberately distort or twist—the process is called *morphing*—a building's elevations into a computer-morphed architectural style.

Currently, the design professions are experimenting with a new delivery process that quite possibly will transform the design professions yet again. Called *offshoring*, it is the practice of using service providers—individuals, branch offices, or other companies—located outside the United States to produce some part of the project work product. The offshored work product can be perspective renderings, computer animation, model making, specification writing, accounting, cost estimating, report production, marketing brochures, and routine computer drafting. Entire preliminary design packages can be sent offshore for the production of construction documents. Even design work is offshored. Architect Kimberly D. Patton, AIA, partner in the Cincinnati design firm of GBBN Architects, commented in the January 2005 issue of *Architectural Record* that, in her opinion, as much as 40 percent of a design project can be offshored.[50]

In my experience, large multidisciplinary design firms can and already do offshore even more than 40 percent of a project. They have been moving design work from office to office for years. It is not much more of a leap to move the work overseas.

I know of an instance where one large design firm was bought by an even larger firm that had an office in India. A particular PM's project was moved from her office in the United States to India. The PM remained in the United States because her local presence was needed to meet with and manage the client. The company moved a key project team member from the PM's office to India for the duration of the project. He became the PM's offshore liaison, in effect her offshore project engineer in the India office. She was regularly on the phone with the project engineer, which required one of them to start work early or stay late because of the time difference. Via a project Web site, she could review drawings in her office that were drawn the night before, in India, while she was sleeping. Because of the time difference, production proceeded at a much quicker pace. Workdays became 16 hours long instead of 8. CADD drafters in India were paid a fraction of what their counterparts in the United States were paid. And there was no overtime! After reviewing the work, she posted her comments on the project Web site and went home. Her counterpart went to work the next morning in India, retrieved her comments from the project Web site and the multidisciplinary, India-based design team continued work on the project while the PM slept.

Offshore design professionals are usually less expensive than their counterparts in the United States. This is the main reason why offshoring is so attractive. Although they may be paid less, offshore design professionals are not necessarily less skilled. World-class and well-trained competent architects, engineers, and planners are located throughout the world. In the same *Architectural Record* article, Michael Jansen, the founder of an India-based production shop, commented that "his firm charges about $150,000 for production work that would cost a U.S. firm $400,000 to do in-house."[51]

Managing offshore projects requires well-thought-out work plans. Expectations must be made very clear. Budget, schedule, and the quality of the work must be monitored regularly. Accurate communications are essential for project success. In the example cited previously, the design firm temporarily relocated the project engineer to the offshore production office. This is not always the case. Sometimes PMs must work via phone and e-mail with individuals in countries where English is their second language. Creating a synergetic design team is very difficult, if not impossible, under these conditions. Offshoring can be a frustrating or rewarding experience depending on the skill, thoroughness, and planning capabilities of the project manager.

Offshoring poses some interesting questions for the design professions that have not, as yet, been adequately answered. For example, have some design profession jobs already moved overseas? Will more move overseas? Is so, what will happen to architectural apprenticeships and engineers-in-training programs in the United States if too many entry-level jobs move overseas? Who will train the overseas design professionals to work with the United States? How does offshoring affect the design professionals' licensing requirement that work be performed directly under their supervision?

These are significant questions with tremendous consequences. How they are answered could dramatically change the design professions and how design projects are managed.

CHAPTER 10 CHECKLIST

Harnessed design teams are only as strong as the sum of their members, while synergetic teams are stronger than the sum of their members. Synergetic teams are the result of a carefully planned working environment. To create this environment, the project manager should ask the following:

❒ Have I empowered the design team so it has the freedom to do its best work?
❒ Have I clearly defined the scope of work?
❒ Have I clearly defined key team members roles and responsibilities?

❏ Do I have a clearly defined work plan with key team member buy-in?

❏ To get buy-in, did I consider holding a group planning session, using a wall chart?

❏ Am I willing to delegate technical decisions to key team members and make the big-picture decisions regarding scope, budget, and schedule myself?

❏ In the project work plan and schedule, have I created a distinct demarcation line between iterative design and linear production?

THE NEXT CHAPTER

Thus far, this book has said little about one of the most important members of the design team—the client. Without the client there would be no project and consequently no design team to manage. Synergetic design teams require clear direction that only comes about if the scope of work is clear and decisions are made in a timely manner. The client is a key contributor to both the project scope of work and decision making. To successfully manage the project and design team, the project manager has to manage the client as well. The next chapter looks at some of the skills a project manager needs to successfully work with clients.

11

CLIENT MANAGEMENT

The architect Louis Sullivan
(1856–1924) lived at the cusp between traditional architecture—also known as classical architecture—and modern architecture. In addition, he worked at a time when his allusive,
nonteam approach to design was becoming increasingly less
appropriate to the design of modern buildings. His most productive years, 1881 to 1895, were spent working as a partner in
the design firm of Adler and Sullivan. Dankmar Adler (1844–
1900) was the more affable of the two and the better business-
man. Sullivan was the iconoclastic temperamental artist, prone
to rapid mood swings. In 1895, Adler retired and Sullivan continued to practice on his own.

The architectural historian Hugh Morrison, in his 1935 bi-
ography entitled *Louis Sullivan: Prophet of Modern Architecture,*
illustrated Sullivan's autocratic and loner-approach to design
and business with a story describing how Sullivan came to design the People's Savings and Loan Association Bank in Sidney,
Ohio:

> [T]he directors [of the bank] outlined for him in informal
> conference their requirements for a new building. The site
> was then an empty corner lot. Sullivan retired to the opposite
> corner, sat on a curbstone for the better part of two whole
> days, smoking innumerable cigarettes. At the end of this time
> he announced to the directors that the design was made in
> his head . . . [He then] proceeded to draw a rapid sketch be-
> fore them, and announced an estimate of the cost.[52]

What Sullivan drew was a modern-looking building, not
typical beaux arts classicism, the style popular at the time.
When one of the directors remarked that he was expecting a
classical-looking building . . .

> Sullivan very brusquely rolled up his sketch and started
> to depart, saying that the directors could get a thousand ar-
> chitects to design a classic bank but only one to design
> them this kind of bank, and that as far as he was concerned,
> it was either the one thing or the other.[53]

Frank Lloyd Wright worked for Adler and Sullivan from the
mid-1880s through the early 1890s. In his book *An Autobiography,* he told a story that illustrated Sullivan's dealings with his
employees. Throughout his life, Wright referred to Sullivan as
"The Master."

> About 10:30 the door opened. Mr. Sullivan walked
> slowly in with a haughty air, handkerchief to his nose. Paid
> no attention to anyone . . . "Here, Wright," lifting a board
> on to my table, "take this drawing of mine. A duffer I fired
> Saturday spoiled it. Re-draw it and ink it in."[54]

Wright continued:

> The Master's very walk . . . bore dangerous resem-
> blance to a strut. He had no respect whatever for a

draughtsman . . . Nor, as far as I could see, respect for anyone else except the big chief—Dankmar Adler . . .[55]

Two things about these stories are relevant to the modern-
day management of design projects. First, Sullivan's haughty,
self-important, Lone Ranger approach to design would be extremely difficult if not impossible to pull off today, given the
complexity of most building projects and the need for a team
approach. Assuming that Sullivan did design the entire People's Savings and Loan Association Bank in his head, he was
then, in effect, the project planner, designer, architect, structural engineer, mechanical engineer, electrical engineer, and
construction cost estimator all rolled into one. One person
with the necessary expertise and licensures to competently and
legally perform all these roles is virtually unheard of today. It
is much more likely that Sullivan worked out the bank design
only conceptually in his head and that the story contains a bit
of hyperbole.

Second, Sullivan's arrogant manner of dealing with his client, the bank directors, would be risky for a modern-day project
manager to attempt. The directors could have easily taken his ei-
ther/or proposition the other way and bid him good-bye. As it
turned out, they did not, but Sullivan was willing to risk the entire job with his self-righteous indignation. Most modern-day
project managers would not dare to jeopardize their projects in
such a cavalier fashion. If today's project manager played the ei-
ther/or card and failed, the design firm could lose the project
and might lose the client forever. Some employees might lose
their jobs as well, the project manager being one of them.

Design firms are businesses as well as design practices that
must make ends meet. Modern design practices and design
projects are not the personal playthings of autocrats, or project
managers.

This does not mean that the customer is always right. While
the adage that the customer is right applies to selling sweaters,
it does not apply to design projects. Sometimes a client needs

to be told or shown what is needed and what is in his or her best interest. Sometimes the news the client needs to hear is not good. The job of delivering the news, good or bad, is the responsibility of the project manager.

To properly manage the project, the project manager must also manage the client. A client's needs and expectations are important. They are the reason for the project in the first place. Satisfying them is crucial to the project's success. Because most design firms rely heavily on repeat work from satisfied clients, the project manager cannot jeopardize this relationship by letting his or her personal agenda put a project at risk.

The truth is, many clients do not know exactly what they want or know what is exactly best for them. Clients frequently speak with many voices and their various representatives have numerous ideas about what they want, with little or no consensus among them. Frequently, the project program that the client envisions is incorrect, inconsistent, contradictory, or incomplete. The design firm's project manager cannot let any of this adversely affect the project.

For a project to succeed, it must have a complete and understandable program. If key pieces of the project program are missing or incorrect, the project manager must work with the client to fill in the missing information and make the necessary corrections.

After the program is determined, a well-defined concept must emerge before proceeding to design development and finally to the production of contract documents. Client buy-in is essential as the process unfolds, or backpeddling may be necessary to obtain client acceptance of design solutions that were developed without it. Many projects have very tight design budgets with only enough money to do things right the first time.

Two common strategies are used to attain early client buy-in. The first is program validation, in which the design firm gets early confirmation that the client's program is complete, correct, and meets the client's needs. The second is the Charrette process, which is used to quickly explore alternative conceptual solutions and obtain immediate client feedback to various alternatives.

PROGRAM VALIDATION

Sometimes a client has a general idea of what it wants before it selects a design professional. It may want a hospital, museum, office building, power plant, water treatment plant, bridge, freeway exit, interior space design, etc. Such projects are frequently described in a program document prepared by the client (or client consultant).

Sometimes there is a considerable time lag between the preparation of the client's program document and when the design process actually begins. In the interim, client needs may have changed. Construction costs may have escalated.

A program validation study evaluates the program document to determine if it is up-to-date and complete and addresses all the factors that will bear on the design. In addition, it validates that the defined project is constructable within the client's budget.

Program validation is an important and crucial first step in many designs. The design process runs much smoother and is more efficient when all the information that affects decision making is available and certain up front. Most clients will recognize the importance of program validation if it is properly explained to them. Program validation goes a long way towards cementing a good and lasting working relationship between the client and the PM because the client sees quickly that the PM has the client's and the project's best interests in mind.

THE CHARRETTE PROCESS

The Charrette process is a tool used for developing the project program and for exploring alternative solutions with clients. Charrette is French for *cart.* Legend has it that during the 19th century, architectural students attending the L'Ecole des Beaux-Arts in Paris worked on their design projects until the last minute, much like students today. The school sent a horse-drawn cart to the student quarters to pick up the design projects. Students who had not completed their assignments hopped on the cart and finished up their drawings on the charrette, the cart.

The name is used today to describe an intense creative and time-constrained workshop during which the project manager and the design team work in concert with the client to resolve program and design problems. The National Charrette Institute (NCI), an organization that is a leader in the promotion of the process, defines the Charrette process as having the following characteristics:

- Charrette is conducted on-site and lasts multiple days.
- The client and design team work collaboratively.
- Teams are multidisciplinary so solutions are cross-functional and integrated.
- Work sessions are short, frequently only a few hours at a time.
- Each work session is followed by feedback discussions.
- Some work sessions address problems holistically, while others concentrate on particularly troubling or important details.
- Progress or outcome is documented and measured and produces a feasible or workable plan.[56]

Prior to the Charrette, the design team and the client researches and prepares. A room in the client's facility is set up as a temporary office, with tables, computers, printer, and fax machine for the key design team members. The Charrette usually begins with a kickoff meeting, attended by the design team and the client's key project user-group representatives and project stakeholders. The Charrette can be led by the PM, client, or a Charrette facilitator. Site and/or facility tours frequently follow. The design team meets with various client representatives throughout the day to discuss their project requirements, needs, and ideas for the project. At the end of the day, a group discussion takes place to talk about the project and the progress made during the day. The Charrette continues with the design team exploring various alternatives and synthesizing ideas and design solutions that show promise.

The Charrette may last several days, depending on the size and complexity of the project. The design team produces drawings, sketches, and diagrams during short work sessions, followed by reviews with the client's various user groups and stakeholders to attain their feedback. On the final day of the Charrette, the design team makes a formal presentation to the client summarizing what was learned during the process. Various alternatives are presented for discussion. After the Charrette, the process and findings are documented. Frequently, the Charrette process produces a conceptual design that is so promising it becomes the basis for further development.

CONTROLLING CLIENT CHANGES

The project manager must control project changes. While the client has the right to make changes, the project manager must tell the client if and how the changes will affect the project schedule, design cost, construction cost, or all three.

Many client-initiated changes are minor. In the interest of maintaining a good relationship with the client, many project managers go along with the requests and make minor changes without any mention of them being out of scope. After all, why risk a good relationship with a client over the design cost of a minor change. Too many small changes, however, can add up and prove quite costly. The phenomenon is called *scope creep* and many projects suffer from it. If not controlled, scope creep can consume a project. It can cause its death, a death by a thousand cuts.

The best way to control scope creep is to address each change as it occurs. If the project manager believes that a client request is not within the scope of work, the PM should tell the client at the time the request is made or as soon as possible. It is my experience that this does not destroy the relationship between the client and the PM. On the contrary, most clients appreciate the candor. Waiting until after the change is made or waiting for weeks to pass before mentioning it *can* jeopardize the relationship.

CLIENTS WITH MULTIPLE VOICES

Some clients have project teams of their own. The teams usually include someone designated as the client's project manager, user-group representatives, and client stakeholders—those with particular interests in the project. In addition, clients sometimes have their own in-house staff of professionals who often contribute to the design of projects. Professionals can include environmental compliance experts, safety officers, engineers, architects, interior designers, space planners, etc.

Members of a client's design team frequently have different interests, opinions, ideas, and concerns. Sometimes these are in conflict. Ideally, it would be nice if the client's PM sorted through competing interests and resolved them before giving instructions to the design team, but, unfortunately this does not always happen.

Sometimes a client project manager appears unable or unwilling to manage his or her in-house team. Perhaps this is because the client PM does not have the clout or the political wherewithall to discipline his or her team and make its members speak with one consistent voice. Instead, they speak with many voices, which are often in conflict.

The design firm's project manager must be wary of client teams that speak with multiple voices. As a general rule, it is wise to take direction only from the client's project manager, not from various client team members. It is best to control communications between design project team members and members of the client's project team. Too many design firm and client team members at various levels giving and receiving information and directions can lead to confusion and inadvertent changes in the scope of work, changes that were never officially sanctioned by either the design firm or the client. Directions and changes that affect the scope of work should funnel through the design firm's and client's project managers.

I remember attending a very unusual project review meeting with a large government agency. The 75 percent submittal had been made about two weeks earlier. The client's project manager had distributed the project drawings and specifications to the client's in-house staff of reviewers: structural, mechanical, and electrical engineers. The client's project manager reviewed the architectural work himself. The client's PM and the three engineers attended the meeting. I brought along my structural, mechanical, and electrical engineers. Each of the client's reviewers brought their comments and marked-up drawings.

The client's PM had not coordinated any of the review comments. Some review comments were mutually exclusive. Because the client had not done any weeding, it was up to me and my design team to tactfully work through the conflicting comments. At one point, one of the conflicting comments was settled in favor of one of the client's engineers over another. The engineer whose comment was not implemented objected vehemently with his PM. An argument ensued. The client's project manager brought the debate to an end as quickly as he could, but the losing engineer got up and stormed out of the conference room. The client's project manager apologized and the review continued.

After a few minutes, the engineer who had stomped out returned with his supervisor, who requested a few words with the client's project manager immediately. Red faced, the client's PM asked us politely to leave, which we gladly did. Although we closed the conference room door behind us, we heard the project manager getting chewed out very loudly.

This story illustrates a practical problem that is rather common among client project managers. They often do not have the political clout within their own organizations to make decisions. Consequently, design firms often receive review comments that are not coordinated. The design firm's PM, along with the design team, must then make decisions for the client. The PM must document decisions made in this fashion and review them with the client's project manager.

PROJECT MANAGER AVAILABILITY

Clients expect project managers to be available and to respond when called. Clients want assurance that their project is being given adequate attention. Clients also expect continuity with the design team and the PM. If the PM is unavailable, sick, or on vacation, most clients expect someone else to step in and manage the project in the PM's absence. It is good to familiarize the client with the individual who will fill in for the PM from time to time.

I remember a project where the person slated to be the project manager decided to leave the firm before a major project got under way. Because of the high-profile nature of the project, the role of PM fell to the office manager. Considerable time was spent making the client comfortable with the new PM. Shortly after this was accomplished, the office manager decided to leave as well. Upper management stepped in and had to spend considerable effort smoothing the client's terribly ruffled feathers.

CHAPTER 11 CHECKLIST

To properly manage a project, the project manager must manage the client, both ethically and professionally. This must not be perceived as manipulation. Most design firms rely on repeat clients for more than 80 percent of their business.

Early client buy-in to the design approach is essential, because most design fees are based on a limited number of revisions. Rework, revisiting, and/or changing program requirements must be kept to a minimum. Two common strategies for achieving early client buy-in to the project process and direction are program validation and the Charrette process. Regarding these two strategies, the project manager should consider the following:

- ❐ Is the client's program clear and complete?
- ❐ Has considerable time elapsed since the program was made? If so, should the program be updated before design begins?
- ❐ Have all the client's user groups and stakeholders accepted the program and does the program meet their needs?
- ❐ Are the client's program and project budget compatible? If not, what can be done to make them so?

It is important to manage client changes. Clients frequently make numerous small changes over the life of a project—scope creep. If not properly managed, scope creep can cause design budget, schedule, and construction cost overruns. The project manager must tell the client the impact of each requested change as it occurs. The project manager should ask:

- ❐ Am I addressing each client-requested change as it occurs?
- ❐ Am I informing the client of each change's design cost, project schedule, and construction cost implications?

THE NEXT CHAPTER

Producing clear, easy-to-understand, and accurate work products—deliverables—goes a long way toward cementing good working relations between the project manager and the client. Work of high quality does not happen by accident. It must be planned and managed. The next chapter discusses project quality control, a major responsibility of the project manager.

12

PROJECT QUALITY CONTROL

Everyone remembers writing term papers for school. Perhaps the first was in grade school, a book report or maybe an essay about "what I want to be when I grow up." Probably everyone remembers staying up late, at least once, the night before the report was due, frantically writing, struggling to get it all down, even counting the number of words. The next morning, the paper was turned in. Remember feeling tired yet relieved and glad that it was finally over?

Sometime shortly thereafter the teacher read everyone's reports, corrected all the spelling, grammar, and punctuation mistakes with a red pencil. She gave all the reports a grade and handed them back. Some students saw all the blood on the first page, grimaced, and looked no further. They shoved the paper into their binder, never to be looked at again. They moved on to the next term paper without learning a thing. The next paper was a repeat and so on and so on.

Others, however, learned something from the teacher's red marks. Before turning in the next paper, they had Mom read it first. Mom found the mistakes before the teacher could and this group of students fixed their mistakes before turning their papers in. The teacher made fewer red marks on these students' papers. Their grades improved. The students and their Moms were very pleased. The Moms may have even said something like, "Johnnie or Jeannie, see how important it is for me to read and correct your homework?"

Most of these students took Mom's advice literally. They had Mom read everything they did, confident that no matter how many mistakes they made, good ol' Mom would find them and fix them. Mom was a great crutch.

A few, however, actually looked at Mom's comments and figured out what they were doing wrong and decided to improve their work themselves. They learned grammar, how to spell, and the proper use of punctuation. They learned to take the time to look words up if they were unsure what they meant or how to spell them. Their attitude about their work began to change. They wanted their work to be as error-free as possible. Their term papers improved dramatically. Oh, they still gave them to Mom to read, but not because Mom was their crutch. Instead, she became their "second set of eyes," a part of the process of preparing a good term paper.

These students realized that having another pair of eyes, a learned pair, with the same noble objective—making the term paper the best it could be—produced far better results than any one set of eyes ever possibly could. When given new assignments, these students started thinking about their papers sooner. They planned them before they started writing. They saw their work as an extension of themselves, a reflection of who they were. They became more methodical in their approach, they paced their work, they monitored their progress, and made sure they gave Mom enough time to read the paper, critique it, and still have enough time left over to pick up Mom's comments.

Each paper improved. With fewer and fewer stupid grammar, spelling, and punctuation mistakes, Mom began focusing more and more on the ideas and content of the paper. Did the paper make sense? Were the ideas expressed clearly, the arguments well developed? Mom now made more substantive comments and the students' grades got better and better.

Among these students who planned their work from the outset, a smaller group still learned to give Mom a preliminary outline of their report to review before they began writing it. These students realized that moving ideas around in outline form was much easier and more efficient than when the entire report was written. Now Mom had the opportunity to make suggestions about how the paper was organized. She could suggest moving major blocks of it around so that the ideas flowed better, made more sense, and had strong beginnings, middles, and ends. These students' grades soared.

These last few students grasped the importance of managing the quality of their work. They learned that quality control is not about finding mistakes afterward. Quality control is about caring enough about one's own work to not make mistakes in the first place. Without knowing it, these students stumbled upon a core tenet of total quality management (TQM). The development of a quality-minded attitude towards everything one does—in effect, having a quality-work ethic—is the lynchpin of TQM.

Something amazing happens when enough people with quality-work ethics band together. The cumulative effect is a quality-work culture. This quality-work culture can spread throughout an entire organization. The quality work–minded infect everyone in the organization who is quality-work challenged. And here is the second fundamental tenet of TQM: infection is free. It is just a matter of the right people doing the infecting.

In his book *Quality Is Free: the Art of Making Quality Certain,* Philip B. Crosby wrote that quality is:

> Getting people to do better all the worthwhile things they ought to be doing anyway.[57]

If one stops to think about it, that does sound like it should be free. After all, shouldn't people be expected to do what they ought to do? Remember the previous story about those few students with quality-work ethics. All that was needed for them to excel was a change in their own attitudes. It cost nothing.

QUALITY-CONTROL CULTURE

For design firms, quality must become cultural. If it does not, there is virtually no way to later fix everything that was done wrong. Relying on a typical quality check (QC) just before the work goes out the door will not work. There might not be enough money for the firm to fix all the problems that poor-quality work can cause once it goes out the door. For design firms, poor-quality work can lead to too many construction change orders, a tarnished reputation, and, ultimately, a loss of clients. Eventually, the world can come crashing in on firms with habitual work of poor quality.

Because quality is cultural, a design firm's upper management must care about quality. They must care enough to have personal quality-work ethics themselves. If they do not, they cannot expect the troops in the trenches to have it, either. Those few employees who do may eventually find the work environment within the firm unrewarding and, out of frustration, choose to work elsewhere. Those good workers that management needs most are the ones most likely to "see the handwriting on the wall" first and choose to leave. Individuals with high-quality standards do not want to fail and much prefer to work with other like-minded people.

To summarize:

- High-quality work cannot be achieved by edict.
- Quality cannot be tagged on at the end.
- Quality is achieved through leadership by example.
- Quality is achieved by developing a firm-wide quality-control culture.

On a firm-wide basis, it is the responsibility of upper management to lead by example. At the project level, the example must come from the project manager. Both the PM and upper management must do more than just preach quality, they must live it. While quality might be free, it must be constantly nurtured.

QUALITY CONTROL AND PROJECT MANAGEMENT GOALS

Clients expect quality products from the design firms they hire. This means a project must meet or exceed all the client's project requirements and expectations. It means preparing accurate and well-coordinated deliverables. It means designing a project that can be bid and built on budget, on time, with few, if any, problems during construction. The purpose of project quality control is to make sure the following goals are being met:

- Meeting or exceeding client requirements and expectations
- Preparing accurate documents (deliverables)
- Finishing the design on time and on budget
- Designing a project that can be built on time and on budget

Notice how well these quality goals mesh with the six goals of project management as discussed in Chapter 2. As a reminder, the six goals are:

1. To reach the end of the project
2. To reach the end on budget
3. To reach the end on time
4. To reach the end safely
5. To reach the end error-free
6. To reach the end meeting everyone's expectations

In fact, they correlate so well it suggests the following axiom: It is not possible to achieve the goals of project management without project quality control.

QUALITY-CONTROL PROCEDURES

Nobody is perfect. It is difficult to check one's own work, because one of the strange things about being human is that we often cannot see our own mistakes. When it comes to quality control, two sets of eyes are better than one.

Quality is not just an auditing process with the aim of producing a record trail. It is not simply redlines on prints. Quality control requires planning right from the beginning. It requires procedures and a commitment by the design firm and all team members to make it happen. It should be part of the project work plan.

Many clients require the design firms they hire to have quality-control programs in place. The State of California's Department of Transportation (Caltrans) is an example. Caltrans requires that:

> The consultant shall have a quality control plan in effect during all project phases. Plans, specifications, calculations, reports, and other items or documents delivered . . . for review shall be clearly addressed in the Quality Control Plan established for the work. The Quality Control Plan shall contain appropriate checklists to assure product quality and control.[58]

A critical point in the design process is the transition from the iterative design phase to the linear production phase. At this juncture, it is wise to do a quality-control check of the design to confirm that it satisfies all the requirements of the client's design program and that no major objectives are missing. The program should be reviewed and the design compared to the program requirements. This review is best conducted by a third-party reviewer, someone not directly involved in the design. Often the design team is so close to the project that things are overlooked because of familiarity.

Some firms conduct formal design reviews at this point. Depending on the size of the project, these reviews may take just an hour or two or may take a full day. The project manager and key team members present the design to the design review team. The review team may include the project's quality-control manager, other PMs, and upper management. Reviewers ask questions and make suggestions.

Other firms use a much less formal approach. Interested staff members gather together at lunchtime. The project manager and perhaps other members of the design team explain the project, the program, and the design response to satisfy the criteria. Input from the brown-bag reviewers is encouraged.

Prior to every submittal, the deliverables should be reviewed for completeness and accuracy. The PM and the quality-control manager must coordinate and conduct the reviews. A discipline check and an interdisciplinary check are required.

The discipline check is conducted by someone with expertise in the particular discipline, usually someone who is not working on the project. Department heads frequently conduct these discipline reviews. Common items checked in a discipline review include drawings, specifications, estimates, reports, and calculations.

An interdisciplinary check is performed by someone with overall experience who looks for conflicts or unresolved items that affect more than one discipline. All deliverables are reviewed for accuracy and consistency with one another. The deliverables are marked up for corrections. The marked-up deliverables are then given to the document's originator for review and concurrence. If concurrence is received, the documents are then corrected—changes, additions, and deletions are made.

Quality-control programs generally require the person making the change to acknowledge that the change has been made, for example, by "yellowing out" the red marks once the corrections are made. The documents are then rechecked against the mark-ups. Marks that are picked up are checked with a checkmark or circled (usually with a colored pencil). If corrections are missed, these are given back to the appropriate team member to make the necessary changes. If no omissions are found, the review process is complete. Figure 12.1 illustrates the process.

Many firms have standardized quality-control checking procedures that are similar to the procedures described previously and illustrated in Figure 12.1. The project manager must make sure that the quality-control process takes place and that it follows the firm's QA/QC procedures. The PM should budget enough hours to perform the review and schedule enough time for it so that the process is meaningful. A quick look at the number of steps suggests that the process can take at least a few days or a few weeks for larger projects. Quality control cannot start on the afternoon of the day the project is due.

FIGURE 12.1   QA/QC Review Process Diagram

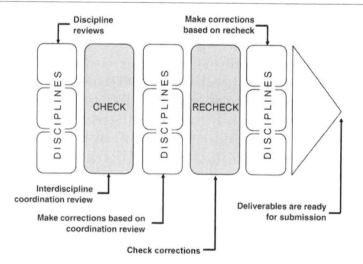

CHAPTER 12 CHECKLIST

The pursuit of quality must be cultural within the design firm. Quality cannot be enforced like a traffic cop blowing a whistle after the mistakes are made. Most projects do not have the time nor the budget to find and fix all mistakes after they are made. Quality starts at the beginning of the project and is based on a quality-work ethic and the consistent following of certain tried-and-proven quality-control procedures. Quality means meeting or exceeding the client's needs and expectations. It means producing deliverables that are as error-free as practically possible.

The project manager must set up the project's quality-control procedures and see to it that they are followed. To this end, the project manager should ask the following:

❒ Have I established a project quality-control program that is consistent with the firm's requirements and procedures?
❒ Have I identified a quality-control manager to assist me in reviewing deliverables prior to every submittal?
❒ Have I allotted ample time for quality-control checking before every submittal?
❒ Before moving from iterative design to linear production, have all the major design issues been resolved to reduce excessive rework that can lead to mistakes?
❒ Do I work in a quality-minded fashion, because I know that as the PM I lead by example?

THE NEXT CHAPTER

As this chapter and previous chapters have illustrated, the project manager has many responsibilities. The PM must manage the project's work planning process, the scope of work, the project's design work, the project team, the client, the project budget, and the schedule. The PM is responsible for creating a work environment that produces a quality experience for the design team, the client, and the design firm, and produces a quality work product that is accurate and complete and meets or exceeds everyone's expectations. It is a formidable job that can benefit from the experiences of others. With this in mind, the next chapter presents some of my project management experiences and insights in the form of simple-to-understand rules of thumb.

13

PROJECT MANAGEMENT RULES OF THUMB

As an apprentice architect, the first rule of thumb I heard had to do with project schedule and quality control. It was said with a big grin, "Never draw more in the morning than you can erase in the afternoon." It is still humorous, although no longer relevant.

Today, with computers and CADD software, construction documents are no longer drawn by hand. It is now possible to erase (delete) an entire drawing with just a click or two of the mouse. If the drawing rule were to be updated, it would go something like, "Never draw more in 7 hours and 59 minutes than you can delete in 1 minute."

In a twisted sort of way, the rule of thumb did make some sense. It guaranteed that by the end of the day, a project would, at least, be no further behind schedule and no less accurate than it was when the day started, as long as all the mistakes and changes drawn in the morning were caught by lunchtime and erased in the afternoon.

Over the years, I learned other rules of thumb. Rules of thumb are important to project managers because they are generally true, practical, and do not require a lot of painstaking analysis to understand and act on them.

Rules of thumb are relatively easy to remember, especially the cleverly worded ones. Project managers often have to make decisions based on incomplete information and hunches. Easy-to-remember rules of thumb can supplement a project manager's instincts. They are helpful in predicting what will go right or wrong if certain things are done or not done. They can foreshadow what will happen long before there is any substantial evidence that it actually is happening, thus giving the project manager ample opportunity to take action well in advance and head off problems before they ever arise.

Here are 14 rules of thumb based on my 30 years of experience managing design projects. Although they are numbered, they are not listed in any order of importance. Seasoned project managers will recognize some of them immediately from their own experiences.

RULE OF THUMB 1: THE LAST 10 PERCENT OF THE PROJECT WILL TAKE 20 PERCENT OF THE BUDGET.

Anybody who has managed at least two projects knows that this is so. It is extremely difficult to finish the last 10 percent of a design project. Remember from Chapter 8 the budget for the hypothetical XYZ project? Recall that 20 percent was budgeted for the last 10 percent.

Clients frequently have 90 percent submittal requirements. This is the clients' last chance to see the documents, review them, and make comments before the documents are complete, stamped, signed, and ready for bidding or construction. Although the project is supposedly 90 percent complete, it rarely is. There are frequently many loose ends—details that are not finished, nasty little cross-referencing problems, and maybe a specification section or two missing.

Maybe the electrical engineer is still working (it seems that electrical is always the last to finish). Maybe somebody forgot to update the list of drawings. Maybe the QA/QC manager did not finish the quality-control check. There may even be coordination issues among disciplines that are still unresolved. This all takes time, meaning labor hours, to correct and finish, and generally, this takes way more than 10 percent of the design budget.

The project manager should plan accordingly. Right from the beginning, 20 percent of the budget should be earmarked to finish the last 10 percent of the work.

Recently, I have noticed that some clients recognize that 90 percent submittals are rarely 90 percent complete and so are requesting a 75 percent or 80 percent submittal instead. While this might help the client rationalize why the project submittal is not complete, this does not necessarily help the project manager. All this means is that when the 75 percent or 80 percent submittal is made, the project manager should have 30 percent to 35 percent of the design budget left.

RULE OF THUMB 2: IF THE SCHEDULE SLIPS, THE PROJECT WILL GO OVER BUDGET.

Project schedules can slip for many reasons. Assuming that the schedule was realistic to begin with, here are a few common reasons why projects fall behind:

- Some project team disciplines were held up because another discipline did not give them the information they needed to proceed on time.
- The design firm, PM, and/or the disciplines do not have sufficient experience with the project type.
- Some tasks were performed by a new consultant or new team member with whom the PM and/or the rest of the project team have not worked.

- The client took too long to perform a particular submittal review.
- The client experienced dissension among its project team and could not make a critical design decision on time.

Regardless of how the project falls behind schedule, this rule of thumb should alert the PM to take corrective measures quickly when the schedule slips, or the project will go over budget. The following example will illustrate why this is so.

Suppose a relatively large multidisciplinary project with a team of 20 is 2 weeks away from making its 90 percent submittal on a lump-sum project. The team has been working for four weeks toward the 90 percent submittal when the electrical discipline lead tells the project manager it needs an additional two weeks to finish. Assume that to this point the project is tracking right on budget. (Remember, the wise PM has budgeted 20 percent for the last 10 percent and has a project contingency.) Assume that the PM phones the client and confirms that it is okay to let the schedule slip by two weeks (nice client). The PM grants the electrical lead a two-week extension and sends out an e-mail telling the design team the new submittal date. There are sighs of relief from various team members because the pressure is off. Everybody keeps working, knowing they have two additional weeks to finish.

By agreeing to the schedule slip the project manager has done more than give the electrical discipline more time to finish. The PM has given the whole project team two more weeks to work on the project! Why? Because when there is a time extension, Rule of Thumb 3, Parkinson's Law, comes into play.

RULE OF THUMB 3: WORK EXPANDS SO AS TO FILL THE TIME AVAILABLE FOR ITS COMPLETION.[59]

As soon as the architects, structural, mechanical, and civil engineers hear about the schedule slip, their attitudes about their own work change. They were once pressing to finish on time, but now they are not. As Cyril Northcote Parkinson pointed out in his 1957 book *Parkinson's Law*:

> [W]ork . . . is elastic in its demands on time . . . [T]he thing to be done swells in importance and complexity in a direct ratio with the time to be spent.[60]

Work slows down, yet everyone is still busy and charging to the job. Some will undoubtedly think of other things to do to make the work better, such as drawing additional details, adding sheet notes, or researching materials just a bit more.

Projects can always be better, if there was just more time. And now there is. Every discipline will expand its work to use the additional two weeks.

This can have a devastating impact on the budget. Assuming an average project labor charge of $90 per hour (a reasonable average job-charge rate for a multidisciplinary office), the project manager had originally budgeted 20 people for 6 weeks, which equals $432,000. If the project manager does nothing, the 20 people now have an additional 80 hours each to work on the job. At $90 per hour, this equals $144,000. The project team will spend $576,000 instead of $432,000, a budget overrun of 33 percent. The PM had better have a healthy contingency fund or else, to use a PM colloquialism, "The project will go into the tank."

The PM should have explored various ways of maintaining the schedule before giving the electrical lead a two-week extension. Some possibilities are:

- Ask the electrical department head if more electrical staff can be added to the project and the schedule held. If so, this is a better course of action. One additional person for 2 weeks (80 hours) at $90 an hour is $7,200, far less than the $144,000 it will cost if the whole team works for an additional 2 weeks. Chances are good that the project contingency can cover this amount.
- Ask the electrical lead whether the schedule problem has to do with electrical engineering or electrical CADD drafting. If it is the latter, there may be a way to get drafting help from another discipline. Multidisciplinary design offices usually have a few CADD drafters who are experienced in several disciplines. These CADD drafters may be busy but perhaps CADD assignments can be jockeyed to solve the electrical lead's drafting problem.
- Ask the electrical lead if electrical team members can work overtime to meet the schedule. If so, the overtime costs that will hit the project will be less than the cost of extending the schedule. Again, the project contingency can probably cover these costs.

If the answer to all these questions is no, then there may be no choice but to grant a time extension. Had this been the 50 percent submittal, the situation might be different. Fifty percent submittals are not usually well defined. The fact that the electrical work is not at 50 percent would not matter. But a 90 percent submittal is a different story. Clients expect all disciplines to be done or nearly done at 90 percent.

The PM can try to convince the rest of the team that a time extension for the electrical discipline does not mean a time extension for all the disciplines. If the office is busy and there are a lot of other pressing jobs, this might work. But chances are, if the schedule slips, the project will go over budget.

RULE OF THUMB 4: IF THE OFFICE IS NOT BUSY, THE PROJECT WILL GO OVER BUDGET.

Almost everyone in an office knows something about the future workload. When things begin to slow down, employees can feel it. Some begin to wonder what will happen next. Some working on projects will begin to milk their work to make it last. Others will look for other project activities that need attention. In his book, Parkinson told a story about an elderly woman with little to do:

> [She] can spend the entire day in writing and dispatching a postcard to her niece at Bognor Regis. An hour will be spent finding the postcard, another in hunting for spectacles, half an hour in a search for the address, an hour and a quarter in composition, and twenty minutes in deciding whether or not to take an umbrella when going to the pillar box in the next street. The total effort that would occupy a busy man for three minutes . . . [takes all day].[61]

The project manager must be among the first to see the slowdown coming and diligently watch and track project progress. If the PM does nothing, the project will go over budget because no one else in the office has any incentive to see the project come to an end. There are no other PMs chomping at the bit to get other projects started.

Projects are much more likely to stay within their budgets when the office is busy with projects waiting in the wings and team members can see their next assignment waiting for them as soon as they are done with their current one.

RULE OF THUMB 5: YOU ARE NOT THOMAS EDISON, SO DON'T REINVENT THE WHEEL.

Of course, Thomas Edison did not invent the wheel, it was the lightbulb, but the point is the same. Architects, engineers, and planners are design professionals, not inventors. PMs should not reinvent the basics. They should stay with tried-and-proven building materials, systems, and methods. Using a material in a different or clever way is one thing. But using a material in an application that is completely at odds with its intended use can cause additional risk to the project. Problems can arise during construction or they can appear later, after the building is occupied. If building materials or systems are used in unconventional ways, clients may not be happy with the results. Manufacturers are likely to not honor their warranties. Their warranties, after all, are based on installing their products as they were intended. Systems may not work and building materials may fail if installed improperly. In the worst case, somebody might get hurt. The following two examples illustrate the point.

Plywood siding is made for vertical applications. It can also be used horizontally at soffit locations, but it should not be subjected to rainwater standing on it or running over its surface.

I recall from many years ago, a project manager who was also the project architect (remember the design studio concept discussed in Chapter 3) invented a new use for plywood. He developed an architectural feature constructed out of plywood siding located over a series of windows. He used textured plywood siding at a 45-degree angle, extending it out above the windows and then returning it 90 degrees to form a 45-degree soffit, which died into the heads of the windows. He called it a "plywood eyebrow." After the building was built and subjected to rain, it did not take long for the plywood eyebrow to develop unsightly gray streaky stains (mold discolorations) and for the 90-degree corner to begin leaking, because rainwater running

FIGURE 13.1   The Collapsed Pyramid

Note the inner core of the pyramid surrounded by the debris of the collapsed outer covering. Photograph courtesy of Werner Forman, Art Resource, NY.

over it also leaked down into the joint. Needless to say, the client was not happy. It was nearly impossible to fix the problem.

Another example is from the distant pages of history. There is an ancient pyramid in Maidum (also spelled Maydum), Egypt. It is the second oldest Egyptian pyramid known to have been built. Its name tells its story. It is called the "Collapsed Pyramid" and it probably failed during construction (ca. 2600 BC). Since then, it has stood throughout time as a pile of rubble and a testament to what can happen when designers experiment (see Figure 13.1). (Not all Egyptologists agree that it collapsed during construction. Some think it may not have collapsed until Roman times. However, for the purposes of this rule of thumb, the assumption is that it failed near completion of construction.)

The very first pyramid was a step pyramid, not a true pyramid with four smooth sides sloping continuously skyward. It is called Djoser's step pyramid, named after the pharaoh who ordered its construction (ca. 2800 BC). It is located in Saqqara, Egypt, about 35 miles north of the Collapsed Pyramid in Maidum.

The architect of Djoser's pyramid was the legendary Imhotep, Djoser's chief vizier. Imhotep designed it as a series of six mastabas (stepped squares) of descending size, sitting one on top of another.

The Collapsed Pyramid was modeled after Imhotep's design, but near its completion its designer or designers decided to experiment. They decided to convert their stepped pyramid into a true pyramid by encasing the stepped structure with smooth limestone blocks sloping skyward at a steeper angle, the precise angle of 52 degrees.

Why 52 degrees? Because the ancient Egyptians were fascinated by their discovery of pi (π). Today every seventh grader knows that pi is the circumference of a circle divided by two times its radius (or diameter). Pi is a constant. It is always the same regardless of the size of the circle and it is an irrational number, meaning it cannot be expressed as the ratio of two integers. The ancient Egyptians discovered pi and were captivated by it, as many people still are today. No one is sure, but the ancient Egyptians may have thought it had eternal or magical powers. Whatever the reason, the designers of the Collapsed Pyramid decided to work it into the very structure of their pyramid.

They did so by likening the perimeter of their pyramid to the circumference of a circle and its height to the radius of the same circle. Having established the base and the height, they computed that the sides must rise at a constant angle of 52 degrees. Pi would then be embedded eternally into the pyramid's very structure. The casing work began and limestone block after limestone block was stacked and fitted in place. As the casing work neared the top, the pressure on the limestone blocks near the bottom was so great it caused them to crumble. The science writer and physicist Bülent Atalay explained that:

[T]he collapse would have occurred so quickly that the workers on its surface would not have had time to escape to safety. Mendelssohn [Kurt Mendelssohn, writer and Egyptologist] suggests that a systematic excavation of the rubble surrounding the exposed tower, the core, may well uncover a large number of buried skeletons still preserved by the dry climate.[62]

The moral of both these stories: experimentation with building materials can lead to serious problems. The project manager of modern design projects is first and foremost a design professional, legally responsible for the health and life safety of the public. Project managers are not systems engineers. A system engineer is someone who anticipates the problems that arise when new technologies/systems are put together in a new way or existing technologies/systems in a unique way. New or novel uses of materials and systems often require tinkering and adjustments to work out the bugs. Sometimes it even requires scrapping the whole project and starting over. A systems engineer oversees this process.

Most clients who hire design professionals are not bargaining for solutions that are so unique that the project is a prototype or experiment requiring the services of a systems engineer to make it work.

A project manager is responsible for the success or failure of the project, not just the management of it. The PM must be wary of those would-be Thomas Edisons who want to experiment. To guard against this, the PM must understand enough about design, building materials, and systems to recognize when they are being used properly and understand the risks involved when they are not.

Most clients and owners of design firms are not interested in turning their projects into laboratory experiments that may or may not work or function properly. Clients who are willing to try something new to solve some unique or unusual problem are the exception, not the rule. Most clients expect things to work and work every time.

As a rule of thumb, design professionals should select building materials, systems, and methods that are tried and proven for their intended use. PMs should not encourage design team members to experiment with or invent new roofing assemblies, new mechanical systems, new flashing details, etc.

I realize that design professionals are a creative lot and that is wonderful. The purpose of this rule of thumb is not to squash creativity. It is to protect against the situation when a team member's creativity crosses the line into unexplored territory, into areas beyond his or her professional training and expertise. Do not confuse creativity with risky experimentation.

RULE OF THUMB 6: IF YOU DO NOT HEAR FROM A CONSULTANT, THE CONSULTANT IS NOT WORKING ON YOUR PROJECT.

The project manager should not assume that no news is good news. If the PM has not heard from a discipline lead for quite some time, the PM should not assume that this is because things are going along smoothly. Chances are that things are not going at all.

Many years ago, I learned this lesson the hard way. A mechanical consultant was supposedly working on the HVAC system for a remodel of an auditorium. Instead, he was really working on another project because that project's project manager had already learned this rule of thumb and was on top of the situation, whereas I was not. Remember the old adage, "It's the squeaky wheel that gets the grease"? It is true.

Eventually, I phoned the mechanical engineer, wondering where the electrical load information was that was promised to the electrical engineer about a week before. It was then that I learned that the mechanical engineer was not working on the project at all.

When consultants are working on projects, they have questions. If the project manager is not getting questions, then it is likely that somebody who should be working is not. It is worth giving the consultant a call to find out the status of the work.

There is a fine line between checking up and badgering. The PM should not badger consultants. No one appreciates badgering and badgering is a poor motivator. But periodic phone calls, e-mails, or visits to check on the status of the work are appropriate. For many consultants, out of sight means out of mind. PMs cannot let consultants forget their projects.

Many years ago, I had an interesting conversation with a principal of an electrical consulting firm. Electrical consultants are notorious for being late. In fairness to them, their work is usually the last to get started and frequently they do not get all the information they need on time to finish their work on time. Often they have to wait to get a finalized reflected ceiling plan from the architect or electrical loads and equipment locations from the mechanical engineer. PMs need to push/encourage disciplines to "feed" the electrical engineer on time.

The conversation with the electrical engineer was about project work. The principal of the electrical consulting firm said that he used to start projects too soon. He would start, and then the architect would make changes that would require him to redo some of his work, for which he was rarely compensated. There is a general tacit agreement between consulting engineering firms and architectural firms to forgive the architects for an unspecified number of minor changes. If a consultant does not honor this unspoken agreement and always asks for additional money for changes, the architectural firm is likely to look elsewhere for an engineering consultant the next time. Consequently, to reduce the amount of rework, this electrical consultant chose to wait as long as possible before starting. "Now," he said with a grin, "I never get started until I hear panic in the project manager's voice."

RULE OF THUMB 7: IF A DESIGN PROJECT HAS NO DEADLINE, WORK WILL CONTINUE UNTIL ONE IS SET.

This rule is a corollary of Rule of Thumb 4. The ideal imaginary project is one with no schedule and no budget. Everyone could work on such a project forever. It would never have to get done and everybody could spend a fortune getting nowhere. Of course, this type of project is a pure fantasy. Real projects have budgets. Because they do, they better have deadlines; that is to say, they must have schedules. Design professionals need deadlines, or they will design forever. They will try out design after design, idea after idea, all the while charging to the project, depleting its budget with no end in sight. The PM must set a schedule at the beginning of the project. If not, work on the project will continue in full accordance with Parkinson's Law until one is set. Waiting too long to set a project schedule will almost certainly guarantee that the project will go over budget.

RULE OF THUMB 8: DESIGNERS NEVER STOP DESIGNING ON THEIR OWN.

Designers love to design. There is never a perfect solution. A good designer can always think of another design that is better than all the others. And once that design is finished, the designer will think of another one that is better even still.

While design and project planning are iterative, production of the contract documents is not. It is linear and for the linear production process to work effectively the design process has to stop. Designers, however, like to continue in the iterative mode, trying out more ideas, revisiting and improving on the design because they believe they can always finesse a design solution into something even better. Many of them will not stop on their own. The project manager must make them quit.

Many years ago I sat at the drafting table behind a designer who was working on a mock courtroom for a law school. After exploring many design alternatives, the designer, the project manager (who was also a firm principal), and the client agreed on a design that seemed to best fit the project's objectives. The client approved the design and the project moved from the iterative design phase into the linear phase of production of construction documents. One morning, about two or three weeks into working drawings, the principal stopped by the designer's desk and was dismayed to see that the designer had out his sketch paper and was busy exploring yet another design. When the principal asked why, the designer explained that he had another idea that seemed to work better than the approved design. He suggested that he and the principal present this one to the client.

The principal lived on antacid pills that he carried around in his pockets. He popped a couple into his mouth and then asked the designer in a very tense voice just how he proposed to pay for all the changes that would result from his nonsolicited new design. "I'll accept cash or a personal check," he bawled and stomped away.

The PM must move the project from an iterative design process to linear production as soon as practically possible. Once production begins, the project cannot turn back to the iterative stage without cost implications, possibly significant ones. Consequently, PMs cannot afford to let designers endlessly explore design alternatives.

RULE OF THUMB 9: THE PERSON WHO TALKS TO THE CLIENT AND DIRECTS THE WORK IS THE PROJECT MANAGER.

I have a general PM survival rule. It is also a good definition to help identify who really is the project manager. The person who talks with the client and coordinates the work of the design team is the project manager. If someone is called the project manager but is not talking directly to the client, then this person is actually somebody else. If the so-called PM is talking to the client but someone else is directing the work and coordinating the disciplines, then the project has two project managers or else— and this is really my point—there is *no* project manager.

Some might argue that this definition is an oversimplification, but, in my 30-plus years of experience, it is not. In the previous example, I would call the person who talks to the client the client manager, not the project manager, because the client manager is not providing the full duties of a project manager. And the person who is directing the work and coordinating the disciplines but not talking with the client? I would call that person the project architect or project engineer or project planner, depending on the type of project. Remember the discussion of project architects/engineers/planners from Chapter 3 and also remember Dr. Stuckenbruck's definition of modern project management theory from Chapter 1, "The project management concept is based on vesting in a single individual the sole authority for planning, resource allocation, direction and control of a single, time-and-budget-limited enterprise."

Project management involves managing the client and managing/coordinating the work and design team. If the duties are split, then there is no clear, and therefore strong, project manager. Along with the split in duties comes the inherent muddling that goes along with the split. The specific duties and responsibilities shared between the two people must be made explicitly clear.

RULE OF THUMB 10: THIS PROJECT IS A "NO CAMPING" AREA.

In this case, "campers" means those charging to the job but not accomplishing anything. Camping out most commonly happens when someone is finished with his or her assignment, but does not tell his or her supervisor so that additional work can be assigned. The person then enjoys office life on the project's nickel.

PMs must know who is working on their projects and what they are supposed to be doing. Progress must be monitored frequently. Most firms have computerized job cost accounting systems that allow project managers to check the status of their projects. Each time-card period, it is possible to see who has been charging to the project. PMs must regularly check their projects' job charges and diligently watch out for those who are camping out on their projects.

RULE OF THUMB 11: FIVE OPINIONS ARE AT LEAST TWO OPINIONS TOO MANY.

Two opinions are sometimes better than one, especially when the second opinion brings additional relevant and useful information to bear on a particular problem. Sometimes three opinions are better than two because the third can be the tie-breaker when a decision has to be made. More than three, however, is usually a formula for inaction.

I have been involved in many projects where the client has had an entire brigade of representatives. Sometimes the brigade has a leader, a spokesperson, or a client-appointed PM who speaks for the group. It is generally the responsibility of the client's PM to take charge and sort out the representatives' various project concerns, desires, wants, and needs and to develop a consensus decision or scope of work on which all of the representatives agree. Often, however, the client's PM cannot or does not do this. It is then up to the design firm's project manager to sort through and make sense of the often conflicting requirements. This can be very time consuming and is often not what was expected when the design fee was negotiated.

I recall a project for a government agency. The project was lump sum and it included a programming validation phase that was to take place before starting design. The purpose of the programming validation meeting was to confirm that the space program, developed by the agency a couple of years earlier, was still valid. I was led to believe during fee negotiations that all that was required was some minor adjustments to the space program.

A meeting was arranged. The client's spokesperson arrived with ten or more client representatives. Early in the meeting it became clear that none of the client representatives had spoken together prior to the meeting. In addition, many of them had significant space program changes to request, some of which conflicted with the requirements of others and some that added considerable square feet to the space program, meaning more costs to the project. Because the client's spokesperson never sorted out the priorities among the different user-group representatives before the meeting, it was up to me, as the design firm's PM, to help do the sorting. Experience told me that this would take more than one meeting. In addition, depending on the outcome, it was going to add considerably to the construction and design costs for the project if everyone got the area increases (and everything else) they wanted.

When the fee proposal is being prepared, it is worth remembering that if client-user groups are going to be involved in finalizing the scope of work, the task of getting a consensus opinion may be very time consuming. The design fee should reflect the added costs associated with doing this.

RULE OF THUMB 12: THE FIRST CONSTRUCTION COST ESTIMATE IS THE ONE THE CLIENT WILL REMEMBER.

This rule of thumb was discussed at length in Chapter 7. It should be clear by now that the first estimate is the most important because it is the one everyone will remember.

RULE OF THUMB 13: DO NOT LET TEAM MEMBERS DISCUSS SCOPE WITH THE CLIENT WITHOUT THE PM PRESENT.

On a recent project for a city agency, an engineering firm had an architectural firm as a consultant. The client and architect had many meetings to discuss the building without the engineering firm's PM in attendance. The result was that many decisions were made that increased the complexity and, therefore, the design and construction costs of the project. In effect, the scope of work changed without the PM realizing what had been agreed to until afterward.

This is not good practice—to let design team members discuss scope with clients without the PM in attendance. It is the PM's job to guard the project against scope creep. The easiest ways to control this is to not let other team members inadvertently agree to do things without the PM's concurrence. Project managers should be in attendance whenever increases in scope are discussed.

RULE OF THUMB 14: THERE IS ALWAYS A PLAN B EVEN IF NO ONE HAS THOUGHT OF IT YET.

As an apprentice architect, when I got stuck on a particular problem, I often sought advice from a very savvy senior architect who sat near me. He must have been able to tell from the look on my face that I had a problem. Often he would smile and before I said anything, he would say, "Do it the other way."

Over the years, I have modified that wise architect's words into a rule of thumb that is a bit more self-explanatory: "There is always a plan B, even if no one has thought of it yet." If plan A is not working, abandon it and go to plan B. If plan B does not exist, then sit down and figure it out, because plan B *does* exist, even if no one has thought of it yet.

I have learned through the years that there is almost never an insurmountable design problem. Design professionals are a very talented and very creative bunch. There is always some other way around a problem, like doing it the other way. An example from American history illustrates the point.

Chicago's Columbian Exhibition of 1893 was held just four years after the Paris World's Fair. The 1889 Exhibition, the centennial celebration of the French Revolution, proved to be extraordinarily successful. Tens of thousands stood in long lines to take an elevator ride to the top of its grandest and most amazing attraction, a 986-foot tower designed by Gustav Eiffel (1832–1923).

The Columbian Exhibition's oversight committee decided that the U.S. fair—the 400th year celebration of Columbus's discovery of America—had to have a tower that surpassed Eiffel's. For the Exhibition's design team, headed by the Chicago-based architect Daniel Burnham (1846-1912), this was plan A.

The 1891 schematic site plan for the fairgrounds, prepared by architects Burnham and John Root (1850–1891) and the landscape architect Frederick Law Olmsted (1822–1903) showed lagoons, meandering pathways, expansive landscaped areas, an area for amusement rides, and a large plaza lined with exhibition buildings. At one end of the plaza was a tower. Although no one on the team knew how to design it, they all knew what the tower was supposed to be, something taller and grander than the Eiffel Tower. The oversight committee quickly approved the plan.

The design and construction of the Columbian Exhibition proceeded at a feverish pace. Dozens of buildings were designed, following the beaux arts classicism style set by the design committee. Swamps were drained and others dredged to form lagoons. Olmsted busily designed the fair's lush landscaping. But nobody tackled the design of the tower. No one knew how. Eventually plan A was abandoned. The Columbian Exhibition of 1893 had no tower.

But it did have a plan B. It had a remarkable contraption that rivaled Eiffel's tower. Hundreds of thousands stood in line and paid 50 cents to ride it. It was a 250-foot-diameter motorized wheel-structure with 36 wooden gondolas that held 60 people each. It was the creation of a Pittsburgh, Pennsylvania, bridge builder named George W. Ferris. Ever since, Ferris's wheel has become the mainstay of fairs everywhere.

Of course, nobody at the time called Ferris's wheel plan B. But it was. There is a lesson in Ferris's wheel for design professionals. After you have gone around and around trying to make plan A work and it will not, remember, there is a plan B—you just haven't thought of it yet. But stay with it, and you will.

14

PROJECT MANAGEMENT CHECKLIST

This chapter summarizes the project management information discussed in the previous chapters in a succinct format for quick reference.

PROJECT MANAGEMENT GOALS AND ACTIVITIES (SEE CHAPTER 2)

There are six goals of project management. They are constant from design project to design project.

1. To reach the end of the project
2. To reach the end on budget
3. To reach the end on time
4. To reach the end safely
5. To reach the end as error-free as possible
6. To reach the end meeting everyone's expectations

All six goals must be satisfied for the project to be perceived as successful by all project stakeholders: the client, the design team, the design firm, and the project manager. The goals of project management should not be confused with project objectives, which vary from project to project.

Project managers have six basic responsibilities. They are the six activities of project management:

1. Defining
2. Planning
3. Directing
4. Coordinating
5. Monitoring
6. Learning

There are five basic phases common to design projects:

1. Start
2. Planning
3. Design
4. Production
5. Closeout

The project manager is responsible for planning the project work and running the project so that all six goals are achieved. To achieve the six goals, the project manager must perform the six activities of project management. To this end, the project manager should ask:

❏ Am I planning, directing, and running the project so it can reach a successful conclusion?
❏ Am I coordinating the design team and monitoring its progress?
❏ Will the project reach the end on budget?
❏ Will it reach the end on time?
❏ Will it reach the end safely?

❏ Will it reach the end as error-free as possible?

❏ Will it reach the end with everyone satisfied and wanting to work together again because the experience was professionally rewarding and met everyone's expectations?

❏ What did I learn from the project and how can I apply what I learned so that the next project will run more smoothly?

THE DESIGN FIRM AND PROJECT MANAGEMENT (SEE CHAPTER 3)

Design firms are organized in four basic ways:

1. Sole proprietorships
2. Design studios
3. Multiple design studio organizations
4. Matrix organizations

There are many detailed variations of these basic organizational structures.

How the firm is managed affects how projects are managed. To successfully manage a project, the project manager must know how the design firm is organized and what is expected of the PM. The project manager should ask the following:

❏ Do I understand the design firm's organizational structure?

❏ Do I understand my position, responsibilities, and duties within it?

❏ Are certain project management responsibilities shared?

❏ If shared, who are they shared with?

❏ If shared, how are they shared? What are mine and what are the project management responsibilities of someone else?

❏ What decisions can I make? What decision must be made by upper management? For example, can I, as PM, make commitments and/or decisions regarding design fees or contract modifications with the client?

CHARACTERISTICS OF A GOOD PROJECT MANAGER (SEE CHAPTER 4)

Project managers are generalists. Good project managers possess the right combination of personality traits and skills. Project managers should assess themselves and ask:

❏ Do I have a high motivation to manage a design team of intelligent, well-educated, creative people?

❏ Do I behave ethically, honestly, and professionally at all times regardless of the temptations to act otherwise?

❏ Do I have the necessary technical background and state licenses to lead this project?

❏ Am I a pragmatist? Am I willing to make decisions based on achieving particular project outcomes?

❏ Will I use all three inference tools of logic—deduction, induction, and abduction—to assist me in making outcome-oriented decisions?

❏ Am I able and willing to make decisions with incomplete information?

❏ Can I enable—empower—the design team?

❏ Do I have a balanced appreciation for the technical, functional, aesthetic, and financial parameters that affect project decision making?

❏ Can I communicate effectively—orally, in writing, and graphically?

❏ Do I strive for perfection but am willing to accept practical compromises?

❏ Am I able and willing to lead, teach, nurture, and coach others?

PLANNING THE PROJECT (SEE CHAPTER 5)

Because "Failing to plan is planning to fail," a project work plan should be developed before beginning every project. The person responsible for developing the work plan is the PM. Two kinds of knowledge are required to properly plan a project: (1) an understanding of project management and (2) the technical knowledge and experience that comes from actually doing design work. The project planning process is iterative, while production task work is linear. There are six objectives of the project work plan:

1. Definition of the project objectives
2. Identification of the project team
3. Breakdown of the project into task budgets
4. Development of the project schedule
5. Establishment of the project quality-control program
6. Identification of other project-specific procedures and standards

Before beginning the project work plan, the PM should ask these questions:

❏ Did I read and do I understand the project contract?
❏ Are the project objectives defined? Were the questions "What, when, who, and how much?" answered?
❏ Are the major parts or phases of the project defined?
❏ Do I have the right design team?
❏ Did I create a project team organization chart and are all the key team members and disciplines identified?
❏ Did I designate a quality-control manager?
❏ Does the project need a CADD manager and if so have I selected one?
❏ Do I need a project controller to assist me in setting up and monitoring project costs using the firm's cost accounting system?

❏ Are the key work tasks identified?

❏ Does every task have an objective, duration, and budget effort?

❏ Did I create a project work plan to document all the project requirements?

❏ Does the project work plan address the following: project objectives, project team organization, project budget and accounting information, project schedule, quality-control procedures, safety procedures, CADD standards, and project filing system?

❏ Did I give the project work plan to all the team members?

❏ If the work plan changed during the course of the work, did I update the work plan and redistribute it to all the key team members?

PROJECT RISK MANAGEMENT
(SEE CHAPTER 6)

Risk is a measure of the amount of uncertainty and potential threats that can adversely affect a project. There are a variety of strategies for managing risk: prevention, transference, mitigation, contingency planning, and assumption. To manage risk, a project manager should consider the following:

❏ Have I and/or the design firm worked with this client before and was the relationship successful?

❏ Have I worked successfully with this design team before?

❏ Is this project of a type and size with which we have experience and were we successful with this type of project before?

❏ Is the project contract based on a nationally recognized standardized contract or is it our firm's standard contract?

❏ Do I understand the provisions of the contract?

❏ Are there clauses in the contract that increase risk, such as indemnity and warranty clauses that require the design firm to indemnify the owner against all claims or warrant work that is beyond the firm's capability to control?

❒ Are there words in the contract that increase risk, such as *certify, ensure, guarantee, insure, maximize, optimize?*

❒ Is the type of fee appropriate for the kind of project?

❒ Is the contract clear or ambiguous regarding what services are included or excluded?

❒ Does the contract specify how disputes are to be resolved?

Here are additional questions the project manager should ask to reduce project risk:

❒ Have I chosen my consultants carefully? Have I successfully worked with them before?

❒ Before I start work on the contract documents is the design well defined and approved by the client?

❒ Do I have an adequate project budget and schedule contingency?

CONSTRUCTION COST CONTROL
(SEE CHAPTER 7)

The project manager must control two different budgets. One is the design budget and the other is the project's construction budget. To control these budgets, it is worth asking:

❒ Did the design team and I put considerable thought into the first construction cost estimate we told the client because it is the one the client will remember most?

❒ Is the estimated construction cost realistic?

❒ Did I develop a budgetary cost model for the project and did I share it with the design team?

❒ Is the design team designing the project within the cost parameters of the cost model?

DESIGN BUDGET CONTROL
(SEE CHAPTER 8)

In addition to controlling the project design and design process, the PM is responsible for controlling the cost of doing the work. The process of establishing a budget for design work is as much art as science. A project's final design budget is generally a nuanced compromise based on many factors, including an understanding of the scope of work, experience with similar past projects, input from the team members who will be doing the work, past experience with the client, and what the market will bear. Design work has a market value. To first establish and then control the design budget, it is worth considering the following:

- ❐ Is the design fee adequate to design the project?
- ❐ If the client says the design fee is too high, is it possible to negotiate the following: reducing the number of design alternatives, reducing the number of submittals, reducing the number of mandatory client meetings, or reducing the scope of work?
- ❐ Have I identified all the project tasks and assigned WBS codes to them?
- ❐ Do the tasks tie into the contract language and phase requirements?
- ❐ Are the WBS codes hierarchical?
- ❐ Is the WBS divided sufficiently to allow me to properly manage and monitor the project? Is it too complicated?
- ❐ Are the task names intuitive so that design team members can easily tell how to charge their time?
- ❐ Am I monitoring the project's financial information frequently enough to take corrective action in a timely manner?

PROJECT SCHEDULE CONTROL
(SEE CHAPTER 9)

Three types of schedules are commonly used by design professionals: milestone list, bar chart (Gantt chart), and critical path method. The project manager should consider the following when setting up the schedule and monitoring the project schedule:

☐ Did I choose the appropriate type of schedule for the project?
  - Milestone list—simple projects with short schedules and few tasks
  - Bar chart—moderately sized and moderately complex projects with no more than a dozen or two tasks
  - CPM—complicated projects with multiple phases and numerous tasks
☐ Does the contract stipulate the type of project schedule? If so, am I using it?
☐ Is there sufficient detail in the schedule so I can properly manage and monitor project progress?
☐ Does the schedule use the same project phase names and task terminology as are used in the contract?
☐ Does the schedule have major milestone due dates that agree with the contract-required due dates?
☐ Have I scheduled sufficient time for quality-control reviews prior to each submittal?
☐ Have I scheduled enough time for client reviews?

Sometimes it is necessary to shorten a project's schedule. To shorten project duration, the PM should consider the following:

☐ Can I run some tasks in parallel?
☐ Can some successor tasks start before predecessor tasks are 100 percent complete?

❏ Are time contingencies built into some of the tasks? If so, can these be reduced?

❏ Can client review periods be shortened?

❏ Would the addition of more staff shorten the time needed to perform certain tasks?

❏ Can the client grant a time extension?

PROJECT TEAM MANAGEMENT
(SEE CHAPTER 10)

Harnessed design teams are only as strong as the sum of their members, while synergetic teams are stronger than the sum of their members. Synergetic teams are the result of a carefully planned working environment. To create this environment, the project manager should ask the following:

❏ Have I empowered the design team so it has the freedom to do its best work?

❏ Have I clearly defined the scope of work?

❏ Have I clearly defined key team members roles and responsibilities?

❏ Do I have a clearly defined work plan with key team member buy-in?

❏ To get buy-in, did I consider holding a group planning session, using the wall chart?

❏ Am I willing to delegate technical decisions to key team members and make the big-picture decisions regarding scope, budget, and schedule myself?

❏ In the project work plan and schedule, have I created a distinct demarcation line between iterative design and linear production?

CLIENT MANAGEMENT (SEE CHAPTER 11)

To properly manage a project, the project manager must manage the client—both ethically and professionally. This must not be perceived as manipulation. Most design firms rely on repeat clients for more than 80 percent of their business.

Early client buy-in to the design approach is essential, because most design fees are based on a limited number of revisions. Rework, revisiting, and/or changing program requirements must be kept to a minimum. Two common strategies for achieving early client buy-in to the project process and direction are program validation and the Charrette process. Regarding these two strategies, the project manager should consider the following:

- ❏ Is the client's program clear and complete?
- ❏ Has considerable time elapsed since the program was made? If so, should the project be updated before design begins?
- ❏ Have all the client's user groups and stakeholders accepted the program and does the program meet their needs?
- ❏ Are the client's program and project budget compatible? If not, what can be done to make them so?

It is important to manage client changes. Clients frequently make numerous small changes over the life of a project, called scope creep. If not properly managed, scope creep can cause design budget, schedule, and construction cost overruns. The project manager must tell the client the impact of each requested change as it occurs. The project manager should ask:

- ❏ Am I addressing every client-requested change as each occurs?
- ❏ Am I informing the client of every change's design cost, project schedule, and construction cost implications?

PROJECT QUALITY CONTROL
(SEE CHAPTER 12)

The pursuit of quality must be cultural within the design firm. Quality cannot be enforced like a traffic cop blowing a whistle after the mistakes are made. Most projects do not have the time or budget to find and fix all mistakes after they are made. Quality starts at the beginning of the project and is based on a quality work ethic and the consistent following of certain tried-and-proven quality-control procedures. Quality means meeting or exceeding the client's needs and expectations. It means producing deliverables that are as error-free as practically possible.

The project manager must set up the project's quality-control procedures and to see to it that they are followed. To this end, the project manager should ask the following:

❑ Have I established a project quality-control program that is consistent with the firm's requirements and procedures?

❑ Have I identified a quality-control manager to assist me in reviewing deliverables prior to every submittal?

❑ Have I allotted ample time for quality-control checking before every submittal?

❑ Before moving from iterative design to linear production, have all the major design issues been resolved to reduce excessive rework that can lead to mistakes?

❑ Do I work in a quality-minded fashion, because I know that as the PM I lead by example?

PROJECT MANAGEMENT RULES OF THUMB
(SEE CHAPTER 13)

Here is a summary of the rules of thumb from Chapter 13.

1. The last 10 percent of the project will take 20 percent of the budget.
2. If the schedule slips, the project will go over budget.
3. Work expands so as to fill the time available for its completion (Parkinson's Law).
4. If the office is not busy, the project will go over budget.
5. You are not Thomas Edison, so don't reinvent the wheel.
6. If you do not hear from a consultant, the consultant is not working on your project.
7. If a design project has no deadline, work will continue until one is set.
8. Designers never stop designing on their own.
9. The person who talks to the client and directs the work is the project manager.
10. This project is a "no camping" area.
11. Five opinions are at least two opinions too many.
12. The first construction cost estimate is the one the client will remember.
13. Do not let team members discuss scope with the client without the PM present.
14. There is always a plan B even if no one has thought of it yet.

PROJECT MANAGEMENT ACRONYMS AND ABBREVIATIONS

Following is a list of acronyms and abbreviations commonly used in project management. Because they are often used without explanation, short descriptions or definitions are given for quick reference.

ACWP   Actual cost of work performed. The amount of money or hours spent performing the task.

BCWP   Budgeted cost of work performed. The amount of the estimated budget earned based on comparing the task work actually completed to the estimated budget for the task.

BCWS   Budgeted cost of work scheduled. The estimated or planned cost to complete a particular task. Can be expressed as dollars or hours.

CPM   Critical path method. The method of project scheduling that graphically shows dependent, interconnected, and related activities or tasks, including the critical sequence of tasks, called the critical path, that must take place on schedule if the overall project is to stay on schedule.

DTC — Design to cost. A method of design in which the initial task sets an appropriate cost target. All subsequent planning, preliminary design, and final design activities and solutions are monitored and tested for conformance with the initial cost target.

FF — Finish-to-finish. Two (or more) tasks are interrelated and scheduled to finish at the same time.

FS — Finish-to-start. Two (or more) tasks are interrelated and one must finish before the other is scheduled to start.

GMP — Guaranteed maximum price. A type of contract with which the design firm invoices on a cost basis up to a stipulated maximum dollar amount that cannot be exceeded.

LS — Lump sum. A type of contract with which the design fee is a specific fixed amount that the design firm receives for its services regardless of how much money it actually spends to provide the services.

MbO — Management by objectives. Method by which projects are managed by objectives rather than by activities or tasks. A set of manageable project objectives are defined. Project progress is then measured by performance toward achieving these objectives rather than by the performance of activities or tasks. Completed work is analyzed and necessary adjustments to future work are made to achieve the stated objectives. The MbO method was first outlined by Peter Drucker in his 1954 book *The Practice of Management*.

NCI   National Charrette Institute. A leading organization that promotes and facilitates the Charrette process. Can be reached at its Web site, *www.charretteinstitute.org.*

ODCs   Other direct costs. A term used in project accounting that refers to miscellaneous costs other than those related to direct labor. In general, ODCs include postage costs, messenger services, printing, photo development, etc.

PERT   Program Evaluation and Review Technique. A work diagramming system that uses statistics to determine the probabilities of task durations.

PM   Project manager. The person who leads the project team. The PM has six main activities: defining the project scope of work, planning the design work, directing the design work, coordinating the work with the client and the design team, monitoring the work progress, and learning from project outcomes to improve performance on the next project.

PMBOK®   *Project Management Body of Knowledge.* The Project Management Institute's guidebook. *PMBOK* is a recognized ANSI standard.

PMI   Project Management Institute. An international organization devoted to the standardization and dissemination of project management knowledge and techniques worldwide and across industry lines. It can be reached at its Web site, *www.pmi.org.*

PMP   Project management professional. A title given to PMI members who have passed a PMI-sponsored accreditation process.

QA/QC   Quality assurance/quality control. Quality assurance involves developing a quality-control plan by which all the "right things" are done throughout the project to achieve a project management process that produces a design and deliverables of high quality. Quality control is the use of a standardized system of checking procedures to ensure that deliverables are as accurate as practically possible.

SF   Start-to-finish. Two (or more) tasks are interrelated so that one task finishes when the other is scheduled to start.

SOW   Scope of work or statement of work.

SREs   Salary-elated expenses. The additional labor costs associated with the employees' salaries such as Social Security, vacation, sick leave, employee benefits such as health insurance, etc.

SS   Start-to-start. Two (or more) tasks are interrelated so that the tasks are scheduled to start at the same time.

T&M   Time and materials. A type of contract with which the design firm is paid for its labor (time) costs and its other direct costs (materials). T&M contracts do not have maximum dollar amounts.

TQM   Total quality management. Involves managing the quality of all aspects of a project including the design, the design process, and the management of the design process. With TQM, a firm's upper management leads by example and assumes that employees will naturally do a good job if properly trained, given the correct tools, and provided with the right overall work environment.

VE   Value engineering. A review and analysis of the design of an architectural, engineering, or planning project by a third-party team of experts with the mission of improving the design's performance, reliability, quality, safety, and life-cycle costs.

WBS   Work breakdown structure. A project work planning tool that divides a project into hierarchical tasks. The highest level or most broad-based tasks are identified first. Each of these broad-based tasks is then further broken down into more specific tasks. Each of these more specific tasks is then broken down until the level of detail necessary to properly control the work is achieved.

Notes

1. Jean-Nicolas-Louis Durand, *Précis of the Lectures on Architecture,* Tr. David Britt, text and documents Ed. Julia Bloomfield, Kurt W. Forster, Harry F. Mallgrave, Thomas F. Reese, Michael S. Roth, and Salvatore Settis (Los Angeles: The Getty Research Institute, 2000), 1–2.
2. Ibid., 84–85.
3. Eugène-Emmanuel Viollet-le-Duc, *The Story of a House,* Tr. George M. Towle (Boston: James R. Osgood and Company, 1874), 10.
4. Ibid.
5. Ibid.
6. Ibid., 123–24.
7. Frederick Winslow Taylor, *The Principles of Scientific Management* (Mineola, N.Y.: Dover Publishing, Inc., 1998), 17. The Dover edition is an unabridged republication of the original book published in 1911 by Harper & Brothers, New York.
8. Stanley E. Portny, *Project Management for Dummies* (Foster City, Calif.: IDG Books Worldwide, 2001), 317.
9. Mary Parker Follett, *The New State (1918),* Chapter II, *http://sunsite.utk.edu/FINS/Mary_Parker_Follett/Fins-MPF-01.html.*
10. Project Management Institute, *A Guide to the Project Management Body of Knowledge (PMBOK),* 3rd Ed. (Newtown Square, Pa.: Project Management Institute, 2004), 23.
11. Linn C. Stuckenbruck, "Project Integration in the Matrix Organization," *Project Management Handbook,* Ed. David I. Cleland and William R. King (New York: Van Nostrand Reinhold Co., 1983), 37–38.

12. Project Management Institute, op. cit., 53.

13. Peirce Edition Project, *The Essential Peirce: Selected Philosophical Writings, Volume 2, 1893–1913* (Bloomington and Indianapolis: Indiana University Press, 1998), 135.

14. Kenneth Allinson, *Getting There by Design* (Woburn, Mass.: Architectural Press, 1997) 94.

15. Ibid.

16. William G. Ramroth, Jr., *Pragmatism and Modern Architecture* (Jefferson, N.C.: McFarland & Company, Inc., 2006), 5.

17. Kenneth Allinson, op. cit., 129.

18. Dana Cuff, *Architecture: The Story of Practice* (Cambridge, Mass.: The MIT Press, 1992), 155.

19. Ibid., 17.

20. James R. Franklin, *Architect's Professional Practice Manual* (New York: McGraw-Hill, 2000), Part 3, 3.7.

21. Dana Cuff, op. cit., 160.

22. Linn C. Stuckenbruck, op. cit., 37.

23. Peter W. G. Morris, "Managing Project Interfaces—Key Points for Project Success," *Project Management Handbook,* Ed. David I. Cleland and William R. King (New York: Van Nostrand Reinhold Co., 1983), 15–16.

24. Kenneth L. Murrell and Mimi Meredith, *Empowering Employees* (New York: McGraw-Hill, 2000), 60.

25. Niccolo Machiavelli, *The Prince* (originally published 1532), *www.constitution.org/mac/prince17.htm,* Chapter 17.

26. John Lloyd Wright, *My Father Who Is on Earth* (Carbondale and Edwardsville: Southern Illinois University Press, 1994), 148–49.

27. Dennis P. Slevin and Jeffrey K. Pinto, "Leadership, Motivation, and the Project Manager," *Project Management Handbook,* 2nd Ed., David I. Cleland and William R. King (New York: Van Nostrand Reinhold Co., 1988), 760–64.

28. State of California 2005 Professional Engineers Act, *www.dca.ca.gov/pels/2005_pe_act.pdf,* paragraph 6703.

29. Excerpt from a typical Federal Government National Park Service (NPS) Task Order agreement for design services.

30. William G. Ramroth, Jr., op. cit., 62.

31. Peirce Edition Project, op. cit., 95.

32. Ibid., 234.

33. Gary R. Heerkens, *Project Management* (New York: McGraw-Hill, 2002), 45.

34. Frank Lloyd Wright Quotations "Truth Against the World," *www.geocities.com/SoHo/1469/flwquote.html.*

35. Excerpt from Henry H. Saylor, *The AIA's First Hundred Years* in "Did You Know," *AIArchitect* 13, February 17, 2006.

36. Arthur Bloch, *Murphy's Law,* 25th Anniversary Ed. (New York: Perigee Books, 2003), 1.

37. Stephen Cassady, *Spanning the Gate: The Golden Gate Bridge* (Santa Rosa, Calif.: Squarebooks Inc., 1986), 15.

38. Richard D. Crowell and Sheila A. Dixon, *DPIC's Contract Guide: A Risk Management Handbook for Architectural, Engineering and Environmental Professionals* (Monterey, Calif.: DPIC Companies, Inc., 1999), VI–15.

39. Stanley J. Strychaz, Ed., *2000 Current Construction Costs* (Chatsworth, Calif.: Saylor Publications, Inc., 2000), III.

40. Charles Jencks, *The Scottish Parliament* (London: Scala Publishers Ltd, 2005), 7.

41. David Cohn, "Scottish Parliament: Enric Miralles's Bittersweet Achievement," *Architectural Record* 02-2005, cover and article 98-111.

42. "Archimedes' Lever," *www.cs.drexel.edu/~crorres/Archimedes/Lever/LeverIntro.html.*

43. Dr. Laurence J. Peter and Raymond Hull, *The Peter Principle* (New York: Bantam Books, 1969), 8.

44. Kenneth Murrell and Mimi Meredith, op. cit., 7.

45. Mary Parker Follett, op. cit.

46. Rensis Likert, *The Human Organization* (New York: McGraw-Hill, 1967), 134.

47. Kenneth Murrell and Mimi Meredith, op. cit., 33.
48. Kenneth Allinson, op. cit., 32, 33.
49. Kenneth Allinson, op. cit., 33.
50. Nancy B. Solomon and Charles Linn, "Are We Exporting Architecture Jobs?" *Architectural Record* 01-2005, 84.
51. Ibid.
52. Hugh Morrison, *Louis Sullivan: Prophet of Modern Architecture* (New York: W. W. Norton & Company, Revised, 1998), 150.
53. Ibid., 150–51.
54. Frank Lloyd Wright, *An Autobiography* (New York: Duell, Sloan and Pearce, 1943) 96.
55. Ibid., 103.
56. National Charrette Institute, "Frequently Asked Questions," *www.charretteinstitute.org/faqs.html.*
57. Philip B. Crosby, *Quality Is Free: The Art of Making Quality Certain* (New York: Mentor, 1980), 3.
58. Caltrans (California Department of Transportation), *www.dot.ca.gov/hq/esc/osfp/project-development/information-and-procedures-guide/manual-sections/1-06.pdf.*
59. C. Northcote Parkinson, *Parkinson's Law* (New York, Ballantine Books, 1957), 15.
60. Ibid., 16.
61. Ibid., 15.
62. Bülent Atalay, *Math and the Mona Lisa* (Washington D.C.: Smithsonian Books, 2004), 65.

This bibliography is an alphabetical listing, by author, of the works quoted or cited. It also includes books, articles, and Internet sources that were consulted while writing this book. This bibliography is not a comprehensive listing of books on the subject of project management nor is it a listing of all the works that influenced the text of this book.

Allinson, Kenneth. *Getting There by Design: An Architect's Guide to Design and Project Management.* Woburn, Mass.: Architectural Press, 1997.

All-Wright Site, "Frank Lloyd Wright Quotations," *www.geocities.com/SoHo/1469/flwquote.html.*

American Institute of Architects, "2004 Code of Ethics and Professional Conduct," *www.aia.org-SiteObjects-files-codeofethics.*

American Institute of Architects, Demkin, Joseph A. Exe. Ed. *The Architects' Handbook of Professional Practice,* 13th Ed. New York: John Wiley & Sons, Inc. 2001.

Atalay, Bülent. *Math and the Mona Lisa.* Washington D.C.: Smithsonian Books, 2004.

Berkun, Scott. *The Art of Project Management.* Sebastopol, Calif.: O'Reilly Media, Inc., 2005.

Bloch, Arthur. *Murphy's Law,* 25th Anniversary Ed. New York: Perigee Books, 2003.

Buckingham, Marcus, and Curt Coffman. *First Break All the Rules: What the World's Greatest Managers Do Differently.* New York: Simon & Schuster, 1999.

Cassady, Stephen. *Spanning the Gate: The Golden Gate Bridge.* Santa Rosa, Calif.: Squarebooks Inc., 1986.

Cleland, David, and William R. King, Eds. *Project Management Handbook.* New York: Van Nostrand Reinhold Co., 1983.

Cleland, David, and William R. King, Eds. *Project Management Handbook,* 2nd Ed. New York: Van Nostrand Reinhold Co., 1988.

Competitive Advantage Consultants, "Partnering Sessions," *www.strategic-change.com/partnering/splash.html.*

Crosby, Philip B. *Quality Is Free: The Art of Making Quality Certain.* New York: Mentor, 1980.

Crowell, Richard D., and Sheila A. Dixon. *DPIC's Contract Guide: A Risk Management Handbook for Architectural, Engineering and Environmental Professionals.* Monterey, Calif.: DPIC Companies, Inc., 1999.

Cuff, Dana. *Architecture: The Story of Practice.* Boston: MIT Press, 1992.

Curtis, Patti, "Offshore Outsourcing: How Far Does It Go?" *Mechanical Engineering–CIME,* January 2005, 24.

Fisher, Roger, and William Ury. *Getting to Yes: Negotiating Agreement without Giving In.* New York: Penguin Books, 1983.

Forsberg, PhD, Kevin; Hal Mooz; and Howard Cotterman. *Visualizing Project Management.* New York: John Wiley & Sons, Inc., 1966.

Franklin, James R. *Architect's Professional Practice Manual.* New York: McGraw-Hill, 2000.

Green, Ronald. *The Architect's Guide to Running a Job*, 6th Ed. London: Architectural Press, 2005.

Hall, Peter. *Great Planning Disasters*, American Ed. Berkeley, Calif.: University of California Press, 1982.

Heerkens, Gary R. *Project Management*. New York: McGraw-Hill, 2002.

Jencks, Charles. *The Scottish Parliament*. London: Scala Publishers Ltd., 2005.

King, Ross. *Brunelleschi's Dome: How a Renaissance Genius Reinvented Architecture*. New York: Penguin Books, 2000.

Likert, Rensis. *The Human Organization*. New York: McGraw-Hill, 1967.

Machiavelli, Niccolo. *The Prince*, 1513. Chapter XVII, *www.constitution.org/mac/prince17.htm*. Considered in the public domain.

Maister, David H. *True Professionalism: The Courage to Care about Your People, Your Clients, and Your Career*. New York: Simon & Schuster, 1997.

Martin, Paula, and Karen Tate. *Getting Started in Project Management*. New York: John Wiley & Sons, Inc., 2001.

Morrison, Hugh. *Louis Sullivan: Prophet of Modern Architecture*. New York: W. W. Norton & Co., Revised Ed. 1998, originally published 1935.

Murrell, Kenneth L., and Mimi Meredith. *Empowering Employees*. New York: McGraw-Hill, 2000.

National Charrette Institute, "Frequently Asked Questions," *www.charretteinstitute.org/faqs.html*.

National Society of Professional Engineers (NSPE), "NSPE Code of Ethics for Engineers," *www.nspe.org/ethics/eh1-code.asp*.

Parkinson, Cyril Northcote. *Parkinson's Law: The Pursuit of Progress.* New York: Ballantine, 1957.

Peirce Edition Project. *The Essential Peirce: Selected Philosophical Writings, Volume 2 (1893–1913).* Bloomington and Indianapolis: Indiana University Press, 1998.

Peter, Laurence J., and Raymond Hull. *The Peter Principle.* New York: Bantam Books, 1969.

Portny, Stanley E. *Project Management for Dummies.* Foster City, Calif.: IDG Books, 2001.

Project Management Institute. CD *A Guide to the Project Management Body of Knowledge (PMBOK),* 3rd Ed. Newtown Square, Pa.: Project Management Institute, 2004.

Solomon, Nancy B., and Charles Linn, "Are We Exporting Architecture Jobs," *Architectural Record* 01.05, 84–90.

Stasiowski, Frank, and David Burstein. *Project Management for the Design Professional: A Handbook for Architects, Engineers and Interior Designers.* New York: Whitney Library of Design, 1982.

Stasiowski, Frank, and David Burstein. *Total Quality Project Management for the Design Firm.* New York: John Wiley & Sons, Inc., 1994.

Taylor, Frederick Winslow. *The Principles of Scientific Management.* Mineola, N.Y.: Dover Publications, Inc., 1998. Originally published: New York: Harper & Brothers, 1911.

Teambulding Inc. Services, "Construction Partnering," *www.teambuildinginc.com/services_construction_partnering.htm.*

Tuchman, Janice L., "Contractor Survey Finds That Specs Don't Measure Up," *Engineering News Record (ENR),* June 17, 1991, 24–27.

Wright, Frank Lloyd. *An Autobiography*. New York: Duell, Sloan and Pearce, 1943.

Wright, Frank Lloyd. *In the Cause of Architecture*. New York: Architectural Record Books, 1975.

Wright, Frank Lloyd. *The Complete 1925 "Wendingen" Series*. New York: Dover Publications, Inc., 1992.

Wright, John Lloyd. *My Father Who Is on Earth*. Carbondale and Edwardsville: Southern Illinois University Press, 1994.

Share the message!

Bulk discounts
Discounts start at only 10 copies and range from 30% to 55% off retail price based on quantity.

Custom publishing
Private label a cover with your organization's name and logo. Or, tailor information to your needs with a custom pamphlet that highlights specific chapters.

Ancillaries
Workshop outlines, videos, and other products are available on select titles.

Dynamic speakers
Engaging authors are available to share their expertise and insight at your event.

Call Kaplan Publishing Corporate Sales at 1-800-621-9621, ext. 4444, or e-mail kaplanpubsales@kaplan.com

PUBLISHING